I0493233

Passive Income:

Develop a Passive Income Empire: Complete Beginner's Guide to Building Riches through Multiple Streams

Simon Wolf

Simon Wolf

paraphrase any part or the content within this book without the consent of the author or copyright owner. Legal action will be pursued if this is breached.

Table of Contents

Simon Wolf

Introduction

The cost of living just continues to go up year in and year out. But, let's face it, our incomes aren't necessarily growing in the same proportion. What happens these days is that many of us need to take on two or three jobs just to be able to save up for the future. In fact, some people need to take on two or three jobs just to survive.

Years ago, a college degree and a good work ethic virtually guaranteed success. Companies offered positions that allowed employees to grow, giving the best workers the opportunity to rise to the top. Flexibility, paid vacations, and a living wage made working one job possible, but in this day and age, companies like this are few and far between. For many, multiple members of the household working multiple jobs is required in order for the family to simply get by.

Unfortunately, all of us have been given the same number of hours every day — 24. If we take on extra jobs, guess what? Our 24 hours remain 24 hours and time for rest and family are compromised.

Sure, working longer hours and more jobs will usually guarantee more income. But a time comes when you may begin asking questions. Is it really worth it? How far do you have to go until the tremendous effort and excruciating labor you invest through your own sweat and hard work begin to outweigh the benefits you reap?

This modern day practice of overworking yourself just to scrape by is a slow killer. Missing out on life experiences, leisure and family milestones just to put food on the table is no way to live. At which point do you stop and realize that the pressure of your commitment renders your income negligible?

While this level of dedication and diligence is most commendable, it is also not very common nowadays. This is exactly why you should look for alternate paths, where your hard work can be aimed at building a business of your own, thus making it finally pay off for you. If you are working ardently at menial jobs that offer little to no room for growth, then it is likely time for you to start focusing those same efforts elsewhere.

The fruits of your work should benefit you, and you first. Think of all the successful people today and all those before them through the ages. Try to imagine what kind of attitude and outlook they had in life. That's right, the answer is obvious. With the exception of those to the manor born, those people were never lazy; they couldn't be. These are individuals who had their priorities right and knew exactly where to direct their energy — into making their business work for them. They chose to build a source of income on their own instead of investing countless hours in a dead-end job never destined to go very far. You shouldn't have to feel that you are investing the only time you have in someone else's business. The majority of companies take advantage of devoted employees. They take the most profit; you are paid a minuscule amount for the work you and your coworkers perform. Eventually, you begin to feel trapped by your superiors and higher-ups. Despite your annoyance with being constantly lorded over and pushed to your limit, you give in to the familiarity, bottom-rung benefits, and guaranteed pay check these jobs have to offer. It is a cozy existence, reliable and boring. Millions of people believe a mundane, monotonous existence is the only road available, but the excitement lies on the road less traveled; the road that is steadily picking up traffic and is begging for you to jump aboard.

You have to ask yourself: Are my days going to be spent on this Earth working for someone else? Or am I going to spend the only life I have on this Earth building a name for myself and my business? We do not realize that a lot of us strive to work under someone for the rest of our lives. Throughout our lives we obey our bosses, doing as they tell us to do because it is corporate policy or because it is part of your job. Wouldn't life be much more rewarding if you could go to work for yourself and make money for yourself by doing and creating things? By building a business of your own?

This is not to say that working for someone is a bad thing; in fact, it is a great way to experience various styles of management. Through experiencing different types of leadership, you can develop your own idea of what good management skills are. When you have the ability to spot good leadership, it much easier to become a good leader yourself. Again, working for someone else is not necessarily bad, but it can also weigh you down over time. Constantly having to do things in certain ways, sometimes outdated ways, just because that's how they "are supposed to be done." Having to fight mercilessly or fill out complex paperwork weeks in advance for a much needed day off. Having your job and livelihood threatened due to something as miniscule as checking your text messages during work hours.

No longer do you have to listen to someone else tell you how to do your job; you can do your own job and make your own money. Not having to walk into the office obeying a dress code, not playing music in the office, not being on your phone in the office – all things of the past. Working for yourself lets you work however is best for you, whenever you want, wherever you want, wearing whatever you want.

Keep in mind that the more successful you feel, the harder you will work, so it is not wise to work in your pajamas or from your bed. Should you choose to work from home, create an office space and wake up at the same time every day and get ready as if you were going out in public.

Adhering to the same standard of dedication to working at home as you would at a regular job will keep you productive. The big difference is that the hard work and time you put in at home will actually help you progress. Set a schedule for yourself, and stick to it. The more you prove your own productivity to yourself, the more effective you will feel and, if you feel successful, chances are you will be successful.

Is there a way to earn more money without having to work more hours every day? Yes, there is. It is called passive income. Of course, this is not a quit-your-job-and-get-rich-right-now type of solution, but a new path to gradually turn to, a path that may very well lead to prosperity, too. A bit of creativity and solid research can take you a long way in this age of information and the truth is that every high-earning business existing now began with the same two ingredients. If you're the kind of person who is frequently brainstorming new ideas, you're already halfway there. Even if you find yourself at loss for creativity, there are many already successful ideas to draw inspiration from. At the risk of sounding too coarse, mere survival is no way to go through life, especially now, when a world of opportunity is right before us.

Passive income simply means you make your money or resources work for you. Passive income, at the core, allows you to earn much money without doing much work. While it may require a bit of effort and time at the beginning, that won't be the case once your passive income system is up and running. You'll be working less and earning more.

Although making a breakthrough and establishing a successful passive income business may be a demanding task at first, it will certainly pay off later. Freedom, independence, and all but full control of your own time are some of the perks of this kind of business venture. Granted, the first steps toward your passive income system will require work, sometimes even hard work, but the end goal makes it all worthwhile. One way of looking at it is this: Within a year's time, with consistent effort, you may be well on your road to both freedom and security. Needless to say, many people work an entire lifetime toward this goal, only to achieve it in old age.

The world in which we find ourselves today is increasingly dominated by technology. Some voices warn of technology "taking over our jobs," marginalizing human effort and work, but they are failing to see the big picture. For someone looking to generate a livable, passive income, technology should be viewed as a friend rather than a foe. The World Wide Web, smart phones, and other technological resources have opened doors to endless opportunity. Just a few years back, creating a passive income and becoming your own boss was feat most people only dreamed of. Now, the Internet and technology have allowed millions of people to break away from the status quo and build their own personal business. Online-based companies like Facebook, Amazon, EBay and more all began with same formula mentioned above: creativity and research. These innovative moguls likely began right where you are now. Who's to say you can't join their ranks using the same technologies they did? What's more, who'd want a back-breaking, painstaking job anyway, if an alternative can be to pull in that currency from the comfort of your armchair? With continuous technological advances come whole new markets and thus a full spectrum of income sources, so easily accessible to millions.

Long gone are the days of the typical 9-5 job, welcoming the new type of job where you can work hard at first and reap the benefits later. Not only does it take a lot of hard work at first, but it also takes a lot of smart decision making. You have to know what you are doing in order to benefit from the many options available; simply going to the website and starting an account won't get you any closer to a life lived via passive income. You have to do the research involved and your hard work will pay off. In reality, technology is not taking away jobs; it is replacing the jobs that require a massive amount of human labor (like plants, manufacturing, warehouses, etc.) and replacing them with safer jobs that do not require as much human risk. The thing you'll be putting on the line with the following methods of developing passive income is your time. The truth is, if you invest enough time in your method, you won't have risked anything at all. The real risk lies in wasting your life and hard work for a company that doesn't appreciate you or your well-being. Technology is changing the way people live and profit for the better. The Internet is giving us ways to make money in a variety of ways without having to go out and look for jobs the traditional way.

Working for yourself and being self-employed is a lot harder than working for someone else. Working for yourself requires dedication and motivation and can't be done by sleeping late every morning and not getting out of your pajamas. Granted, some people who work from home work in their pajamas, but this is not a productive practice. If you are dressed for success, it can help push you to be successful. While we can enjoy the benefits of working from home, or anywhere we please for that matter, we have to keep ourselves motivated by taking the proper steps and doing the proper research in order to be successful.

In particular, we'll be looking at online sources of passive income in this book. You'll learn to do so via Kindle self-publishing, Amazon FBA, niche websites, affiliate marketing, email marketing, and online courses on Udemy. These systems do not need much capital investment. Many do not require an initial financial investment at all. You'll just need to put in the work at the beginning and cruise thereafter when all's up and running.

Back when we were just kids, a lot of us were taught that it is better to do our homework as soon as we got home. Why? Because that way we would have more time for playing later, and we would have no worries about our obligations ruining our fun. Not to mention that there would be none of those unpleasant moments when time's running out, and you find yourself knee-deep in assignments.

Well, passive income is a lot like doing your homework as soon as you're home. You will put in the work right away, but with the aim of having more time to relax later. Nothing worth having comes easily; work hard now so you can relax and enjoy the benefits of your hard work later on in life and throughout your self-employment. With every success comes a great deal of hard work and with every minute of hard work come financial rewards that you earned for yourself, on your terms, benefitting you.

So are you ready? If you are, turn the page and let's begin.

Simon Wolf

Chapter 1
Passive Income 101

Passive income is money that you earn without doing much work or working significantly less, i.e., while being "passive." Active income is the salary you earn from being employed. Passive income is interest on your bank deposits or investments in Treasury bills. Active income is the professional fee you earn for rendering consultancy services. Passive income is earning rental income from the apartment unit you're leasing out. It is money dripping into your pocket from an (ideally) autonomous system you have established.

Active requires work. Passive requires little or none at all, once established.

They say it is more work to work for yourself than it is to work for someone else. This is true. Working for yourself requires a high degree of self-discipline, dedication, and motivation. It is empowering to work for yourself, but it can also be significantly more stressful because any mistakes made are on you and the only one who can fix them is you. When you are the boss, you are responsible for the business. When the business is your livelihood, this adds a whole new weight of stress. Through the stress and frustration that employing yourself can shroud you in there comes a large sense of pride and self-worth because you created something successful and are sustaining yourself in this world because of it. It was once hard to believe that working for oneself could be done so easily with a computer and a telephone, whereas now it is more common to see people working from home or working for themselves than it is to see people employed full-time at another organization.

Gaining active employment is also less work than setting up your passive income platform. This is another way in which the two differ: With an active income job, the work begins after you become involved in the process. On the other hand, with passive income, most of the work comes at the start, while you're still building the business; after that the idea is to work less and less over time. The two choices develop in opposite directions, as you can see, but they both serve to reach the same goal — making money.

The key advantage of passive income is that, with some effort and ideas, you can end up earning more, even much more, than you would in an average, regular job. At the very least, you should reach the point where your income is equal to that of an average job, but you will still be working significantly less! At the very most, your income will exceed that of a normal job, giving you extra time and financial freedom to live your life the way you desire; not behind a desk.

THE FORMULA

Earning passive income is not instant. In fact, it may seem ironic but it actually requires a lot of hard work. But this hard work is mostly confined to the beginning and, once the system's up and running, you'll hardly ever need to work, especially if you let other people manage it for you. So, without pre-empting the discussion, I present to you the passive income formula.

Creation

Only God can create something from nothing. You can't. So, if you want to create passive income, you need to have the materials you need to build it with — a system.

This is where most, if not all, of the hard work, time, and resources are very much needed, because this is the foundation. Have you ever seen a building being constructed? Probably 70% of the construction time is spent on the foundations. In fact, that's why we think buildings are relatively fast to build — the construction of everything else above the foundation is quick once a solid foundation is in place, which takes time.

It is the same with your online passive income systems. You need to set up the right systems and set them right if you are to consistently earn passive income. You can't squeeze blood from the air and therefore you'll need to create something — a product or service to sell.

In addition to effort and diligence, which are really crucial, you should see this as the part where any and all creativity you have may be most beneficial. Do not be afraid to consider your own ideas as possible recipes for success, but do be cautious. Your personal hopes and visions for the kind of business you want to start may be hard to capitalize on, so be prepared to make compromises to maximize your chances of success. At the same time, that one idea you've had for the longest time somewhere in the back of your head may, in fact, have the perfect place on the mountain of opportunity that is the Internet. The best way to successfully adapt is through market study and tons of research, because information is power. Armed with the info and a thorough understanding of the markets you want to break into, your next step will be to experiment.

Experimentation

Given that you're new at this, you'll find that you do not know everything perfectly — or well at all! You will also need to take risks and experiment to see what works. The key here is not to eliminate risks — that's impossible — but to manage them well. Experiment by taking well-calculated risks and you'll be able to fine-tune what you've created so that it can generate consistently passive income for you. Obviously, this is where information and awareness come into play and do their part to minimize the likelihood of failure. If you exercise due caution, the experimentation will be harmless; you'll get to adjust your business with minimal to no risk.

As important as experimentation itself is being safe while you're at it. Keep in mind that methods and markets discussed in this book should usually require little to no financial investment to get you started. This means you should beware of opportunities that may pop up out of thin air, promising towers and castles for just a little, or not so little money. Naturally, it is up to you how much money you want to allocate to your own venture, but always remember that easy streets are rare or non-existent.

There is nothing huge to gain in this world without putting in a high degree of work and time, unless you win the lottery or gain an inheritance. In terms of business and making a name for yourself and keeping the name afloat, this requires a great deal of dedication and discipline. Learning what you are good at and terrible at is part of learning about yourself. Through experimentation, you can find out what you love, what you hate, and what you are naturally good at. Some people choose niches based on their talent or their ability to do or research the niche, while others pick niches simply out of interest and desire to either learn more about it or to share their knowledge about it with the world.

After trying out a few different things and seeing a few results — good or bad — things should begin coming into focus. At this stage, certain options will start to look better than others, and you should have a much better idea of your choices and opportunities to seize. Remain thorough when inspecting the pros and cons of each prospect. An attractive advantage in one place shouldn't draw you there if there's also an underlying catch.

Elimination and Addition

Through experimentation, you'll discover what works and what doesn't, and you'll see what else you need to add. This also helps you to discover what you find interesting and what you do not. It is hard to stay motivated and passionate about something if you lack interest in it. At this point, you'll need to eliminate those things that not only do not work but are keeping your passive online system from taking off and running like a well-oiled machine. You may also need to augment it with things that you haven't considered at the beginning. Fine-tuning is important to set up a consistent passive income system.

Unfortunately, this part of the process may mean that the time has come to ditch certain ideas and expectations. Compromises really aren't a bad thing, though, and you may even find that learning to let go of certain original ideas is liberating, especially if they hold your project down. Of course, sometimes just improving upon those ideas may be all that you need to do, and you will certainly see ways in which you can do this as you progress.

Your efforts to shape the most profitable means of passive income should also make apparent what you need to add to the mix. If a certain approach is a no-go, further experimentation is sure to show you the way. If you're really hung up on an idea and do not want to give up that easily, try out a few different approaches and adjustments. But you have to know that some models are just not feasible, and that's okay.

Delegation

Not everyone is a techno-geek. Chances are that you aren't, either. There will be times when you need to delegate tasks and responsibilities to other people so you can concentrate on what's more important in terms of running your online passive income system. Why spend a month trying to figure out how to shoot a good video course to sell when you can hire someone to shoot it for you so you can concentrate on making the course's materials excellent? By delegating, you'll also get to leverage other people's expertise.

Many websites make it is easier than ever to employ the services of a freelancer on virtually any task! From payment and deadlines to the specific needs of your particular operation, anything can be negotiated. While you do need to get well acquainted with their actual skills and abilities, hiring a freelancer is definitely another step toward your kicking back and letting your passive income start flowing.

The prominent websites that offer freelancer services will have various systems to ensure your investments are not squandered. Later in the book, we'll take a look at some of these sites, which are trusted and renowned throughout the Internet. Exercising due caution and making good use of their policies on client protection is a ticket to successfully getting others to do your work for you. After allocating your work and consolidating your operation in this regard, the time comes to look at even more ways in which technology will serve you.

Automation

This is the fun part. When you've set your system up very well and have delegated the tasks to key people, you can use technology to automate most of the processes — if not the whole process — and have more time for more important things in life, such as family, friends, or watching your favorite "Friends" re-runs.

There are a lot of ways to go about automating many aspects of a huge variety of endeavors along your way. Whether you're dealing in affiliate marketing, all kinds of sales, or managing your website(s), technology will come in handy time and time again. Later on, as we go through the many means of passive income on the Internet, we'll look into just how technology will make your life a whole lot easier within specific operations.

ADVANCES IN STRATEGIES

Because of the web and its many social media platforms, work and contracting platforms, and a variety of other advances, there are more ways than ever to make money passively. There are hundreds of different avenues for making passive income and having a constant flow of profits coming in. Granted, a lot of work and research is needed initially, but it is possible to create a recurring, passive income for oneself after the effort is put in.

The huge amount of technology in today's society, along with the use of tablets and smartphones, allows you to check and monitor your business from nearly everywhere. Radiologists can read x-rays and MRI's on their telephones, and IT professionals can fix servers from hundreds of miles away. It is a large and connected world we live in now, and it is important that we take advantage of that in the business aspect.

WAYS TO EARN PASSIVE INCOME ONLINE

In the succeeding chapters, we'll take a good look at some of the top ways you can start earning passive income via the Internet. These are Kindle self-publishing, Amazon FBA, niche website marketing, affiliate marketing, email marketing, and online courses like Udemy. Even wider than the range of different sectors open for business on the Internet, is the number of ways in which you can approach each of them! With a lot of opportunities also come quite a few things to look out for, though. Whether you should look to avoid or grab them, we're about to cover them.

Earning income online is easier than it ever has been before. You can sit at your computer and browse the Internet and probably find hundreds of ways to make money in the scope of several hours. These are real, tried and true ways to make money through the Internet, not scams filled with false promises. Granted, there are a lot of scams on the Internet, but you have to know how to weed out the scams and know what is too good to be true. With the use of so many different forms of social media and websites, individuals can make money in places such as Snapchat, YouTube, Instagram, Facebook, Twitter, Tumblr – and the list goes on. Anywhere there is a high amount of traffic, there is a potential to make an income. Think of it as a road; if you set up a fruit stand on the side of a busy street corner, you will be seen by thousands of people in a day and get a lot of customers.

If you set up your shop on the side of a dead road, you may get a few customers, but you won't get nearly as many people seeing you. People who see you on the busy road may not stop that same day to purchase something, but they may be back, or they may tell their friends, families, and coworkers. The importance of word of mouth, especially on the Internet, is very important. You can see how just being seen once can have an impact and reach lots of people; just imagine how many people you can reach through the Internet: millions. That's right, millions.

If you want to be seen, you need to know where to park and what to sell; the term "sell" can be used literally or figuratively. You need to use the Internet and all of its facets to create a passive income that gives you the freedom to be self-employed and the financial stability that everyone desires. Being able to pay bills with money you have generated by your own hard work for your own business is like eating salad from the garden you planted: delicious. Do not for one second think this book is going to teach you how to take handouts and how to make money online easily. Everything in this book takes a large amount of work and research upfront in order to enjoy the benefits of your work afterward. As with everything, "work hard, play harder"; use that slogan to get you through the hard days, and you will use your hard-earned money to play on the good days.

Without further ado, let's get into it.

Simon Wolf

Chapter 2
Kindle Publishing

Kindle Direct Publishing is a platform on which you can self-publish your books for free. Kindle Direct Publishing, or KDP, is Amazon's self-publishing platform that allows you to easily publish your own books, maintaining complete control over them while at the same time reaching out to millions and millions of readers worldwide.

Yet another shining example of the way the Internet paves the way for millions of ambitious people, Kindle publishing opens up the writing market like never before. Whatever your targeted field may be, from novels to manuals, there is virtually no limit to potential success. With Amazon's far-stretching global reach, audiences worldwide can quickly be introduced to your content.

The aforementioned control over your content is one of the key benefits of this system. What this means is that editing, formatting, cover design, etc., are up to you, and you only, to guide and organize the way you see fit.

With Kindle direct publishing, you can earn royalties on your work of as much as 70% of the cover price. KDP also gives you the ability to publish quickly, making your books available on the Kindle Store within a few hours or even minutes upon uploading of your material. Can you imagine how unbelievable this would have been a couple of decades ago, or even more recently? There is nothing stopping you from publishing a book within minutes, for millions to have instant access to! I mean, getting your work published, let alone making it so available, used to be a real headache for writers. Well, that time is no more.

KDP gives you the opportunity to market your books to millions and millions of readers worldwide with the presence of Amazon.com in practically all countries. Lastly, KDP allows you to make your books available for everyone, as ebooks that can be read through Kindle devices and free Kindle apps while caring for the environment.

WHY KINDLE SELF-PUBLISHING?

Self-publishing, as a means of passive income, is becoming even more popular these days. There are a couple of reasons for this. First, most of the obstacles or entry barriers that normally face new businesses do not exist in self-publishing. What this means is that, to self-publish your books on Kindle, you do not need specialized software, you do not need to be an authority figure, expert, or guru on the particular subject that you want to write about, you do not need to do network marketing or be connected to influencers, you do not even need to sell to people directly or address a market, and you do not need to spend a whole lot of money. In fact, it is possible to earn from Kindle self-publishing without having to spend anything more than the cost of your Internet connection.

As a matter of fact, not even substandard quality of your written content will necessarily preclude you from making money from it. Certainly, you should always dedicate your best efforts to producing quality, but this may not be the actual determining factor in particular niches or specific target audiences. Depending on the field you want to cover, your potential readers may care more about the gist of the writing, rather than academic prowess or lingual expertise.

The fact that it is so simple to get into self-publishing on Kindle also means much less risk or, rather, the freedom to take more risks than you could in the traditional publishing world. This is because these platforms are not very demanding investment-wise and allow much more room for experimentation and trying out different niches, approaches, and styles.

Another reason for the rising popularity of self-publishing is that it provides a very good opportunity to earn good passive income. After you've written your bestselling book and uploaded it to Amazon.com's Kindle Store, you simply wait for sales to trickle in.

Lastly, this can give you a huge opportunity for achieving fame and good income. Considering that Amazon is present in practically all countries all over the world in the millions of people who buy books on the Kindle Store, you have a sea of opportunities for success.

HOW TO SELF-PUBLISH YOUR FIRST KINDLE EBOOK

Research

The first step to successfully self-publishing your first Kindle ebook is to do your research. The odds of successfully publishing your first ebook, as well as subsequent ebooks on the Kindle Store, depends largely on your ability to find the right niche or topics to cover.

Many self-publishers make the potentially fatal mistake of assuming that topics they are very much interested or passionate about or topics that they strongly feel will be ahead will be very good topics to self-publish books about. Now, I'm not saying that such topics are doomed to automatic failure. While it is good if you can publish on something that you are very interested or passionate about, there's more to successfully self-publishing a book than writing on such topics.

The key to determining if a potential niche will be profitable in self-publishing is to choose topics that many people are interested in. By researching first what people want, you practically eliminate the chance of failing on your first self-publishing attempt. This is because you will be self-publishing based on a model that has worked for all businesses since time immemorial — supply and demand.

So, when doing your research, it is important to look for patterns in the place where you will be selling your self-published ebooks — the Amazon Kindle Store. What is it specifically that you should look for in terms of patterns?

First, look at the books that cover or focus on the same topic or niche. Next, evaluate the positions of these and other similar books within the context of the overall sales of the Kindle Store as well as the top 100 bestsellers in their categories. Finally, look for a market place or niche that is not yet crowded because those are the ones you have a significantly higher chance of dominating and succeeding in. Though the average person may believe choosing a broad, widely liked topic is best, widely liked topics are often already oversaturated with content. Finding a specific sought-out topic is the key.

Here is a list of examples of niche topics that have found success in the Kindle Store:

- Anti-aging

- Antiquing

- Astronomy

- Backpacking

- Bass fishing

- Beauty

- Camping

- Chess

- Cheerleading

- Classic Cars

- Credit Problems

- Decorating

- Divorce

- Dog Training

- Gambling

- Gardening

- Golf

- Hiking

- Horse Racing

- Hunting

- Interior Design

- Investing

- Knitting

- Landscaping

- Life Coaching

- Magic Tricks

- Mental Health

- Motherhood

- Organic Food

- Parenting

- Photography

- Pregnancy

- Quilting

- Rafting

- Real Estate

- Relationships

- Scuba Diving

- Self-Sustainability

- Skin Care

- Time Management

- Travel

- UFOs

- Volleyball

- Weight Loss

- Woodworking

- Yoga

Of course, you are not tied to any one of these topics. These are simply listed here to inspire you or spark an idea. If it is possible to reconcile that which is in demand with the content you really want to write, then that's even better. However, the market may often dictate that you completely abandon certain ideas and force you to adapt to the supply-demand dynamics of the market.

Now, this is just the start. As much as you can significantly increase the chances of successfully publishing your first ebook on the Kindle Store — and by successfully I mean earning income — it is not a guarantee. You'll next need to come up with a good book that's worth your market's time and money. And the first thing you'll need to do in order to accomplish that, regardless of whether you'll be the one to write the book yourself or hire someone else to do it, is...

Outline

Creating an outline for your self-published ebook can go a long way in helping you write one that is very easy to read as well as understand. Nothing else can sabotage your self-published ebook more than being scattered and unorganized. By creating a good outline, you minimize the risk of coming up with an ebook of poor quality and significantly increase your chances of self-publishing a high-quality one. Outlining also makes it much easier for you to write your ebook.

So how do you go about creating a very good outline for your first self-published ebook? For starters, you can start with the table of contents of the books you evaluated earlier. The beautiful thing with Amazon's Kindle Store is that it allows you to take a sneak peek inside the books it sells. You can check out those books' tables of contents so that you can have an idea of what you need to cover for your particular topic. It can also give you an idea, if you are well versed on the topic or have done enough research for it, of what is missing from most of these books so that you can cover them in yours.

When creating a book, a good way to start is to find a template online or to create one yourself. You do not necessarily have to come up with a title now, but you can create an outline and simply scribble "Title" at the top. In your outline, the easiest way to go about laying it out is to start with either a "prologue" or and "intro," depending on the type of book you are writing. This is not necessary, but a lot of people like to read intros because they can provide a lot of background information on the topic that is to be discussed.

Then, start with "Chapter One" and scribble out some main bullet points that you want to cover in the chapter. If you are aiming to have a book with 20,000 words, you can divvy up the word count evenly among the chapters, so you know how much you need to write for each; this method works for some, not others. After scribbling out the bullet points, you can do the same for the rest of the chapters until your book is concluded. You may or may not need to rewrite your outline, depending on how much scribbling you did. An outline is a great trial-and-error device because it gives you a good framework for your book, essentially the skeleton, and it keeps you moving as you write the book and make it from one bullet point to the next.

Other people are able to "wing it" and go at it without an outline. Most of the time, these people burn out around halfway and never come back to the book. This is a risk you have to take. Unfortunately, sometimes it takes longer than a few weeks to write a book; sometimes it takes years, even decades. It is incredibly stressful to write a book without an outline because you will come to many points in the book where your thoughts will jumble about where to go next and what direction the story should go – outlines allow you to stop, take a deep breath and look at the outline. Scribble down the thoughts rolling around in your head and keep moving. For the visual readers, here is a good example of an outline:

<u>Title</u>

- Potential ideas

<u>Intro/Prologue</u>

- Ideas
- Ideas
- Ideas

<u>Chapter 1:</u>

- Ideas
- Ideas
- Ideas

<u>Chapter 2:</u>

- Ideas
- Ideas

- Ideas

And so on, until you are out of ideas. The structure is used to avoid chaos, business plans are used to keep businesses stable and going in the right direction; children learn to outline their essays in school so they can write an effective paper; and writers outline their books so they can write effective, interesting books that are enjoyable to read.

The review section is another useful resource for creating your outline. Consider both the negative and positive reviews, but pay more attention to the negative ones. Negative reviews give you important insights into the weaknesses of books that have been published in the same niche or on the same topic that you can fill in or exploit. Essentially, negative reviews can help you avoid pitfalls that can sabotage your outline.

Positive reviews give you insights into what other books have done right, what your potential readers will appreciate best, and, of course, what ideas to further build on. You do not necessarily have to reinvent the wheel, but you can make the existing wheel much better and succeed in self-publishing your first ebook on the Kindle Store.

Finally, after the groundwork has been laid down through sufficient research, and an idea of the demands has been clarified by looking at reviews, it is time to move on to the main work.

Write the Book

Now that you have created your outline, it is time to write the book. You can do this in two ways: Hire a ghostwriter or write it yourself.

If finding time to actually write a book, good writing skills, and expertise on a certain topic or niche are serious challenges for you, then hiring a ghostwriter is the way to go. No, I'm not talking about hiring Casper the Friendly Ghost or some other spooky elements, but real people who can actually write well on your chosen niche or topics and are willing to transfer all rights to the written work to you. In other words, ghostwriters are people who are willing to write your book for you and give all credit, financial and otherwise, to you in exchange for a fixed payment. You'll publish the book under your name and get all the glory, fame, and, hopefully, royalties.

If you are worried about the potential direction that the ghostwriter may take your book, you can start it off with as many, or as few words as you like and write out where you would like the book to go. You can state what you do not want to be included in the book and what you do want to be included so that they have a better understanding of what you want and what you expect from them. There is a lot of flexibility when it comes to dictating the outcome and direction of your book.

So where can you hire ghostwriters who'll do the dirty work for you? There are many websites you can check out, such as Upwork (formerly known as Odesk/Elance) and Freelancer.com, among others. Hiring ghostwriters is very easy. The challenge lies in hiring good ones. You will have to do due diligence and maybe even ask for legitimate samples of their work in order for you to screen out the good writers from the bad ones.

One way you can have an idea whether or not a prospective ghostwriter is good is by looking at the client feedback section in their profiles. There, you can see how their past clients feel about the quality of their work. In the same section, you can get an idea of their average rating. You can also see how well they communicate back and forth with their past clients, reviews from past clients, and their average success rating.

Another way to get an idea of a perspective ghostwriter's caliber is by checking out how long have they been writing or working for clients in the website as well as how many gigs they worked on already, if such information is possible or available. It is a good way to gauge how much writing experience they already have.

Keep in mind that quality always comes at a price. As such, prospective writers that charge rates that are ridiculously low — compared to most others, at least — may be having a hard time getting enough clients to make a living one way or the other. While it is not a guarantee of poor writing skills, chances are their writing may not be of high enough quality or that they do not have enough experience yet. Either way, it is your choice — and risk.

There is also the risk that you will hire individuals who believe they have a high degree of skill and charge a high rate, only for you to find out the hard way that they really have little experience. Speak with the client, observe their grammar and how they interact with you. This will give you a good idea of how reliable and talented the client is. Also, do not be afraid to ask for samples from the client.

The more prominent freelance websites, such as Upwork, for example, can help you attract the breed of writer most fitting for your budget. While setting up your project, it is possible to provide specifics concerning your situation and resources. The level of experience you are looking for or are able to pay for can be presented in the description. What this means is that you can point out that you're willing to accept less experience, but for less pay, and vice versa. This serves to better illustrate your conditions and needs to all potential writers.

Granted that a risk comes with buying these services, follow the steps mentioned above and that risk becomes minimal.

Cover and Title

Two very critical aspects of your ebook are the title and cover. While it is true that it is what's inside that counts, your cover and title are the features that will entice people to at least check out the content by either "looking" inside or downloading a sample. These two are the doors through which people need to enter in order to see your book's content. If the door's unattractive, they won't even consider peeking inside.

Both your cover and title must stand out and be different, i.e., eye-catching. Given that the average prospect on Kindle has limited time to choose and tons of other books to sort through, they'll most probably pour over the available books on Kindle quickly and as such, your book only has a second — probably even a split-second — to persuade readers to interrupt their searching to check out your book's contents or descriptions.

Consider using eye-catching photos or vivid colors that make you stop and look. Do not use photos you picked off the Internet, use those you have taken yourself or purchased through stock photography. Using other people's photos on the cover of your book is a form of plagiarism and could also break copyright laws. Anything that makes the potential audience stop and look is a great choice. It also needs to be relevant to the title or at least add a degree of ambiguity to make the audience want to read more.

You want the reader to want to read more and a catchy title is a good way to do this. You can pick the title either before or after your book is written, but a lot of times it is best to choose the title afterward because, as you write your book, you may head in a different direction than the title suggests, which could prove to be misleading to the reader. Try to give your book a title that hasn't been used before, which can be difficult if your topic is about something very common; it is a bit easier if you are writing fiction.

Contrary to traditional wisdom, people will indeed judge a book by its cover, and they'll judge it quickly. Given that your ebook has quality content, the cover and the title will definitely captivate and pull in the vast majority of your potential readers. Whatever one tries to sell in life, the importance of visual appeal can never be neglected. Not only is the initial appeal essential, but it can prove very advantageous. Many things have been sold solely on first glance, often regardless of the inner values! That, of course, doesn't mean that you should sell nicely packaged but horrible content; after all, in the writer's market, you have to mind feedback.

The best way to create a great cover is to get professional help. Fortunately, it doesn't cost much to get great book covers done these days. You can outsource from websites like Fiverr, where all gigs are standard-priced at $5.00. The important thing is you already have an idea of what you'd like the cover to be about, so the graphic artist can easily do the cover per your specifications. If not, it may take a little bit of time and going back and forth to get right.

Once you get the cover done, it is time to work on your title. The title gives readers an idea of what your book is all about in just a couple of seconds. This is where great copywriting comes into play. Good copywriting can help you relay to your potential buyers what your book's about, which will be the main criterion by which they'll decide whether or not to buy your book.

Some good tips to make your title stand out and grab the readers' attention and convince them to at least check out your book's Amazon page and sample include:

- The title must identify the main benefit of reading the book, like weight loss or better health, for example;

- The title must be specific in terms of benefits identified, like "Increase Sales by 100% in 1 month.";
and

- The title must be keyword-rich so that it will rank well in searches for certain keywords in Amazon because the first step for getting noticed is being seen and if your book doesn't rank well in Amazon searches for your niche's or topic's keywords, the probability of it being seen is very low if not nil.

If word play is not your strong suit, it is again possible to employ the services of a freelancer, this time a copywriter, who has a very strong grip on magically arranging words. For a minimal investment, you will give your book an effective title, which may subsequently prove crucial in capitalizing on your work. I have witnessed clients setting up projects and contests on freelance websites, looking for copywriters to brainstorm on their company name or slogan in exchange for a prize or a small fee.

<u>Description</u>

Your book's description can make or break your book's success. While the cover and title entice people to take a peek at your book, your book description can give them a clear picture of what to expect from your book. It can also give readers that strong push toward checking your book out further by downloading a sample of it and reading the reviews, if any.

This is also the part where there is room for creativity and clever writing, but do not ever lose sight of your goal — pulling in the customers! Relative to the theme or genre of your book, various tactics may be appropriate to spark interest among readers. If the book is a work of creative storytelling, perhaps a thriller element will work well in your description. On the other hand, if it is a more instructive or educational piece, it may be a good idea to keep very clearly to the point and core of the content. Given that consumers are hasty and usually impatient in their searches, it may also be important to remain concise, as most people can't be bothered to read a long and vague description.

Your book's description is practically your main sales page and, as such, it is a great idea to learn some copywriting techniques and principles to increase its chances of enticing readers to buy your book or download a sample at the very least. Do it well and you'll be able to convince people to buy your book. Do it poorly—well, you get the picture.

Legal Protection

To protect your personal economic interests in your book, you should have it copyrighted. While any originally created work is automatically protected by copyright in the United States, that's not the case for other countries. Therefore, it is still best to register with the local copyright office of your country of residence outside the States. Even in the United States, the initial copyright has no laws preventing co-creation. If another person or organization writes the same book as you do and publishes it before you, you have no legal protection if you cannot prove the first publisher read your work.

The simplest and fastest way to go about copyrighting your work is by logging on to copyright.gov. Copyright.gov is a site run and operated by the Library of Congress. Registering your intellectual property for a copyright is a fairly simple and inexpensive process. Once you are on the site, a simple form will allow you to register your work, pay the fee and move on. Once you have your copyright in order, you will be legally protected from your work being stolen.

Due to the vastness of this market, there will always be a few people who may want to steal your work. The worst part is that they may actually succeed in making money off it and, with sufficient marketing skill, even surpass your own success. Of course, Kindle has systems in place to prevent content theft, but this will only protect you so far. It is always better to go the extra mile and establish a solid copyright protection for all your work. Better safe than sorry.

Price

People want to get the most value for their money. While it is true that content is what ultimately gives people value, they still want to get that value at a certain price. This is the reason why, despite being one of the best if not the best phones in the world, not everyone who wants an iPhone actually buys one. For many people, the price tag is just not commensurate with the quality. They work on a budget.

It is paramount that you optimize your price well, especially in the beginning. Once you start selling, your income, as well as your feedback, will tell you if the price can be increased or must be decreased. Regardless, you should make every effort to get it right at the very start in order to maximize your performance on the market.

So what's the ideal price for your ebooks? First consideration is the market. Most Kindle ebooks are priced between $0.99 and $2.99 for an ebook that's about 10,000-15,000 words on average, so you may want to price somewhere in that range.

Speaking of market, another good way to price your books is by considering the prices of similar books in your niche or market, especially the bestselling ones. This should give you an idea of what the market may think the value of your ebook will be. Looking into the competition and paying close attention to the way they do things is always profitable. When it comes to prices, the average pricing in your field should be well understood and explored. This will show you where and how you can take advantage. Sometimes, taking your price a little under that of the competitors might just give you the edge you need. At the same time, if you know you've got premium content, then this information will tell you just how far you can take it without overpricing your product.

The second consideration is your desired royalty income. Pricing your ebooks between $2.99 to $9.99 gives you a royalty income of 70% of the price per unit of sales while pricing it outside that range — higher or lower — reduces it to just 35%. For maximum royalty income, the sweet spot therefore is the $2.99 to $9.99 range.

Publish

Now that your book is done, the last frontier is to simply publish it on Amazon's Kindle Store. The writers of the past would have thought you lost your mind if you told them that, in the future, there would be a marketplace where publishing is actually the easiest step! Gone are the days of needing a publisher in order to publish your work for the world to read; a decade ago, this would have been unbelievable. Just follow the instructions on the website, which are pretty easy to follow, and wait for it to be approved and available for purchase at the Kindle Store. It is that easy!

Simon Wolf

Promote

While it is not entirely necessary, promoting your book can significantly help boost sales. You have several options available, both paid and free. You can always use your social media accounts like Facebook and Twitter to promote your book for free. Sometimes, the best way for books to gain popularity is by word of mouth. If friends and family read your book and come back to you for more material, you know you wrote a good book that is likely to gain a good return. Should your family and friends fall in love with the book, ask that they recommend it to their friends and family either with or without an incentive for doing so.

If your friends and family are receptive to your book, kindly ask them to leave a review. The more positive reviews left on your ebook, the more traction your book will receive. More reviews also help to drive your book up in search result rankings. For example, if a reader is searching for a romantic novel and your book has generated numerous positive reviews, it will likely come up more quickly in a search, driving traffic and attracting interested readers.

Another great way to promote your book is by submitting it to blogs that focus on books reviews or those that are centered around your niche topic. For example, if you write a book about intermittent fasting, you may want to submit it to a dieting blog or a weight loss blog. If you write a book on backpacking through Europe, try submitting your book to a travel blog. If you write a work of fiction, try finding a blog that focuses on your genre.

Starting your own blog is another great way to promote yourself as an author and curate a brand. Once you discover your niche topic, whether it be dieting, gardening, or romantic fiction, start a blog that details your own background. Share articles related to your topic and include a link to your book for the readers. Post updates on new books you have in the works and even ask those reading your blog what topics they would like to see books about. By keeping a current blog, you will likely build up a following and through this, you will generate even more paid readers.

Besides Facebook, other free social media outlets are great for unpaid promotion. Many authors congregate on Twitter, where they are able to share tips with each other, promote each other's work and gain access to the attention of more avid readers.

A seemingly small but enticing gesture to encourage readers to purchase your book is to offer a free chapter. Kindle allows authors to do this. Allowing people to read the first chapter of your book free of charge will often draw them in and leave them wanting more. Much like a movie trailer attracts interested viewers, a free teaser chapter attracts intrigued readers.

For paid alternatives, you can use Facebook advertisements as well as outsourcing it via websites like Fiverr.com, among others. There are many paid outlets for promotion, including ad space on websites and email marketing. There are endless resources when it comes to online promotion.

ADVANCES IN STRATEGIES

While publishing a book on Kindle may seem relatively straightforward and arguably simple, keep in mind the difference between professionally published books and most self-published books. The process of creating, editing, and publishing a book made sure that the final print version was free of grammatical errors and filled with interesting content, beautiful sentence structure, and easy-to-read verbiage. When you self-publish on sites such as Kindle, you are essentially your own writer, editor, and publisher. What you produce and publish to the Internet is under your name and is a reflection of your ability as a writer.

Keeping this in mind, make sure that everything you publish is perfect in terms of grammar, word usage, sentence structure, verb tense, etc. Individuals can read a book and enjoy it, then spot an error that could eventually lead them to write a bad review or not recommend this book to friends and family. When you are first starting out, read your book, re-read it, have two other people read it, and then re-read it again before publishing. Know how to take criticism because, being a writer, you will receive criticism.

Also, make sure that what you are writing about is something that is popular or something that, if you were shopping for a book, you would purchase if you came across it. You want to produce the highest-quality work, especially when you are first starting off and gaining an audience. Publishing on Kindle, although "easy," doesn't mean you should go and write a bunch of short stories in one day and publish them that night. Take your time and re-read to the point of ridiculousness and once you are 110% sure your book is ready to be published, do it.

Once you get the hang of it, do not be afraid to let your Kindle business progress. As you continue publishing content and garnering avid readers, you can begin outsourcing other writers and forming a team. Even if you write yourself, utilize quality ghostwriters to boost your speed in content releasing. Eventually, you can have others running your business for you, or you'll be producing "evergreen" content that continues to bring in income months or even years after it is been released.

Chapter 3
Amazon FBA

Amazon FBA (fulfilled by Amazon) is a program that lets you sell your goods on Amazon's online store. Fulfilling orders is possibly the biggest challenge facing many online entrepreneurs but, with FBA, it is a breeze. You can simply store your products with Amazon, who'll take care of the logistical stuff such as warehousing, shipping to buyers, handling after-sales concerns, and providing great customer service. This frees up a lot of your time to focus on what really matters — providing great, value-for-money products to customers.

It may be clear by now that Amazon is among the front-runners when it comes to ushering in new and highly accessible business opportunities for virtually anyone to benefit from, and then some. The FBA program is a glorious example of just how much technology, particularly the Internet, positively affects our ability to establish our own businesses. Just consider how much you can improve and consolidate your business venture if you are unburdened of the most demanding tasks at hand, which, as I've stated, are usually the logistics.

The new vacancy in your schedule will provide ample time for procuring products and expanding the variety of your assortment, setting up relationships with quality suppliers, etc. Needless to say, this is an obvious and enormous advantage from the very get-go, when compared to other means of online sales. It is incredible to realize that we live in a time where a small business, as small as a hobby even, can simply sign up and begin cooperating with the conglomerate that is Amazon. And not only cooperate, but directly reap the benefits of their powerful establishment to advance your own income.

Another thing worth mentioning is that this system will serve you just as well if your goals are not all that high. What I mean by this is that FBA can also be used to simply liberate yourself to spend the free time on things other than your online business. Once you have established a satisfactory amount of consistent income from your sales, you may want to just lie back for the most part and let the money dribble in, turning your income into truly passive income.

As mentioned before, most of the required management or intervention in your business can be automated or delegated to other people. In the course of building your passive income system on FBA, you'll see for yourself the ways in which your specific operation can become more and more autonomous.

AMAZON FBA VS. AN ONLINE STORE

Aside from who's handling the logistical stuff, there are other reasons why Amazon FBA is superior to setting up and managing your own online store. First is faster delivery. With Amazon's extensive market reach and logistical capabilities, it doesn't take long for your stuff to get to your customers. Contrast this with doing the shipping yourself. Not only will this help to better satisfy your customers, but fast shipping also expands the array of products you can sell. Time-sensitive goods that may expire, or otherwise suffer due to prolonged shipping processes, offer one such example. Quick shipments, with a guarantee of such an enormous enterprise, make for an advantage hard to earn when you're out there by yourself.

Second, FBA gives your products significantly more exposure than if you promote them on your own. That's because Amazon is the biggest online retailer in the world — even bigger than most physical retailers! By having your products on Amazon FBA, you enjoy much higher visibility and, potentially, significantly more sales than you would in your own online store. Of course, complete independence may have an appeal, but setting up shop and making a name for yourself may take years upon years of hard work and commitment. Apart from being exhausting, the risks and possibilities of failure if you're going it alone are substantially higher. Since you are reading a book on passive income, you probably aren't very enthusiastic about the whole prospect of putting years of work into a venture that may not even pay itself off.

Third, making your products available on Amazon's FBA allows your customers to take advantage of its free shipping within two days and other similar delivery options. Again, this is a logistical advantage you can leverage to sell more of your products efficiently. Furthermore, this and other advantages offered to customers on Amazon are among the reasons that this platform enjoys such a wide consumer base throughout the globe. This is exactly how this universally beneficial system operates in a way that provides all parties their slice of the cake.

Lastly, FBA gives you — as an online seller — much needed credibility because, simply put, Amazon is one of the most trusted brands in the world. Can you imagine how beneficial it is to piggyback on the reputation of one such as Amazon? Lovely, is not it? This brings us back to the subject of making a name for yourself as an online retailer, as this step is pretty much not an issue on FBA. Naturally, you still want to get positive feedback and ensure a satisfied customer base, but the degree to which FBA facilitates this process for you is truly invaluable. Should any issues arise after the shipment, Amazon's highly professional staff will handle their end in customer services to deal with any potential complaints or misgivings. As far as buyers are concerned, they are dealing primarily with Amazon, while you come into play as a third party that offers the products and is vouched for by the renowned Amazon company.

SETTING UP YOUR FBA BUSINESS

It is not rocket science to set up your own FBA business and start earning passive income. It'll take some work, though. As is the case with most other passive income sources, it is all about building a solid foundation for your FBA business. Here are the steps toward enjoying passive income via Amazon FBA:

- Account: Sign up for a professional account to maximize seller benefits.

- Niche: Research what niche is best to get into and generate ideas on what products to sell on FBA. Some niches are definitely profitable while others are trash, so research well. This means some quality market study and analysis until you get a good grasp of the supply-demand climate in a particular niche, as well as the nature of the competition therein.

- Suppliers: After determining what particular niche and products to sell on FBA, you'll need to find a good supplier. A good supplier is one that doesn't just provide quality products but also delivers on time — even ahead of schedule. When looking for the right supplier, consider asking for samples, determining a good lead time, and estimate your potential margins on the products.

- Listing: Once you've found a great supplier, you should make a listing for your chosen product on FBA. Use good keywords and great content to make your product page the best that it can be. Popular keywords and search engine-optimized descriptive content often play a big role in attracting potential customers. If SEO writing and handling keywords successfully are tasks you find difficult, this is also something that can be delegated to a freelancer.

- Traffic: Once everything's been set up and is running, the last frontier is to make more people aware of your product page on FBA to bring them there. You can do this in many ways, both free and paid. Your free options are social media and word of mouth, while you can place paid advertisements on Facebook and other websites.

PRODUCT IS KEY

Selling the right product is the single most critical factor for succeeding on FBA. These are usually cheaper, easily shipped products with minimal risks associated with transport. Your products should be known far and wide as goods that arrive fast and in the promised condition. This is harder to achieve with certain kinds of products, so be mindful of what you want to get into, especially in the beginning! So what are the things to consider in order to arrive at the "right" product? These include, among others:

- Price: Ideally, the products should be within the $10 to $50 range. This type of product sells the most and is the easiest to sell. This range is pretty much always more or less a sure ticket to success, so naturally it marks the right place to start your business.

- Weight: Your products must weigh as little as possible, mostly because lighter products will cost you less for shipping, storing, etc. Cheaper logistics are not the only reason to go for light products, though. The less they weigh, the less likely they are to be fragile, so the possibility of any potential problems with transport is greatly reduced.

- Competition: Like anywhere else where selling takes place, FBA is a competitive marketplace. Determine if you have any actual and potential product competition within the top 5,000 best-seller rank (BSR) in your product's primary category. Also, make sure that you do not have competition from branded names in your chosen niche or category, as this is a very potent competition killer. It is always a good idea to stay away from the big fish, especially if you're the new kid on the block. Overcrowded, monopolized, or otherwise full markets or niches are another thing to avoid.

- You must also check out the reviews the competition has received. The more reviews they have, especially positive ones, the greater the competition and, consequently, the challenge of breaking into the market. If there are fewer than 50 reviews of competing products, it indicates a pretty good chance of cracking that niche or market.

- Toughness: Whenever possible, sell products that do not easily break. This will minimize your risks for refunds or replacements, both of which can significantly affect your margins. Consider the distances your goods might have to travel to get to the customer, as well as the means of transport required. Always calculate the risk involved in dealing with certain products, as some of them are a nightmare to ship. The smoother the shipping is, the more solid your base of income will become.

- Margins: Ideally, your margin (percentage of profit over selling price) must be at least 75% to make it worth your while. Always keep an eye on the numbers, because this is the lifeblood of your business.

FBA SUCCESS

The top sellers on Amazon are outliers, i.e., way different and separate from the rest of the pack. They tend to adopt the thinking that selling on Amazon is akin to stock market or currencies trading. More than that, the following factors have — to a great extent — accounted for their success:

- Economies of Scale: Selling more of a product is more cost-efficient — and profitable — than selling a few. Selling on Amazon makes economies of scale much easier, as the logistics are handled by a leading logistics behemoth. This is why smaller price ranges are a highway to success on FBA, and I stress "highway"! Once your system is up and running, these products will sell fast and in large volumes. And in the process of getting up and running, well, obviously it is easier to amass a customer base by selling numerous cheap products.

- Objectivity: The ability and willingness to be accountable for errors in judgment and adjusting accordingly is key to being flexible and successful in the arena that's called Amazon. Behaving in the opposite way just makes it impossible for sellers to do the right thing at the right time for selling success on Amazon. Not everything goes according to plan all the time. This is completely normal. The trick is to learn from your mistakes, be responsible and keep going. Perhaps most important, you must have the ability to self-criticize and see the errors of your ways clearly and on your own. These virtues will help you understand when and how to adapt and improve your business, and this is crucial to success.

- Discipline: The most successful sellers are disciplined enough to control their inventories, cash flows, and risks very well. If you are taking care of business personally, it is important to be meticulous and well organized. Think of it as managing a store, which is exactly what you're doing, essentially.

- Focus: Maintaining a clear focus on your goal and having stone-hard will and determination. This is how we get places in life, and it is no different on FBA. The top Amazon sellers do not care about being right or wrong — they just care about making money. Lots of it!

- Time Frame: The most successful sellers view things in longer time frames, such as quarters or years, instead of days or weeks only. Even in other walks of life and business, this is the way that the vast majority of successful people think. It shows that you are thinking big, are ambitious and see the big picture. This kind of perception of time also helps you look forward with great foresight, which is a great organizational skill.

If you carefully and wisely consider these factors in starting your Amazon FBA business, you significantly increase your chances of making good money.

ADVANCES IN STRATEGIES

When deciding to start selling through Amazon, know that it is not usually as simple as buying a bunch of cheap products and reselling them on Amazon. Find a niche and stick to it, do not attempt to sell a variety of products all at once because that will be far too much overhead. For example, say you want to sell phone cases. This is a very popular item on Amazon so, in order to stand out, browse through some of the most popular Amazon phone case stores to see the types of phone cases offered, the styles they sell the most of and that are most popular, and the type of phones they sell for.

Doing this gives you an edge in the business because you can see what's popular and what has worked in the past, and use that knowledge to search for products that are similar and better. The worst thing you can do is sell the exact same products as someone else, because this saturates the market and kills business for both companies. I am not saying cell phone cases would necessarily be a good market to get into, because the market is already overloaded with hundreds of different options, but it is a good example of a niche market. Other markets could be nail polish, women's clothing, greeting cards, etc. There is an endless amount of markets to choose from; just make sure you pay attention to what is popular, what is not, and read the reviews on the most popular and least popular items to get an idea of what exactly the customer does and doesn't like.

A good question to ask is, "Would you buy the product"? If you were searching online for the product you are selling, knowing what you know about the product, would you be willing to purchase the item for the price listed and still be pleased with the product? If the answer is yes, then wonderful. If the answer is no, you should look for another item. You want to sell quality items at good prices; people will know when the items they purchase are cheap. Angry customers and incredibly satisfied customers are the most likely to leave reviews, so make sure you strive to satisfy.

Simon Wolf

Chapter 4
Niche Websites

A niche website is one that's focused on a very particular target or term, normally referred to as "keywords," which are what search engines like Google and Bing use to help people look for stuff on the Internet. And for your online passive income purposes, it is best that your niche website's keyword is very particular, unique, or focused.

WHY A NICHE WEBSITE?

One reason you may want to put up a niche website for passive income purposes is that it is relatively practical, i.e., cheap, to get up and running. If you'd like to speed up the process, you can pay for services and products that can help you do that but generally speaking, the only compulsory cost involved is for getting a domain name and a web hosting account, which averages between $5 and $7 monthly, depending on your choice of host.

While it may take some time and lots of work to set up your niche site, it is not complicated at all. The relative simplicity of setting it up is another good reason to get into niche website marketing.

Yet another good reason is the results timeline. While it is true that nothing will make you money overnight, niche website is much faster in terms of driving traffic and generating income, compared to blogging, which may take you months or even years to build up enough of an audience to make good money.

Lastly, niche website marketing is one of the most passive of passive online incomes. In fact, it is possible for you to reach a point where it can run on autopilot while it generates income for you, leaving you with more time for other stuff like life or putting up other niche websites. Yes, it may take time and work but, once it is up and running, you can just let it be.

It would be irresponsible of me not to come clean about the other side of niche website marketing, i.e., why other people aren't drawn to it or shun it. First is that it is not a genie-ATM-in-the-bottle or slot machine. As mentioned earlier, you will have to put in the time and effort, especially when it comes to setting up the website. Moreover, it is not going to generate instant income, contrary to what others would have you believe. Not only does it take time to set up your site and everything it needs to work, it'll also take time for Google to actually notice your content and rank your website in search results for its niche keywords and for meaningful traffic to come to your site.

While you can earn good income from niche website marketing, it is one that may be quite limited. The giveaway here is the word "niche," which means position and implies a high degree of specialization or focus. As a result, you have fewer prospects compared to more generalized products that have much larger markets. While it is certainly possible for you to turn your niche site into an authority on your particular niche, the chances are pretty low and eventually your income potential can plateau. You can mitigate this risk by setting up other niche websites, which you can do with the amount of free time that you may enjoy once your niche website's already up and running.

HOW TO SET UP YOUR NICHE WEBSITE

As I wrote earlier, setting up a niche website may be a bit time-consuming and require some amount of work but it is relatively simple to do. Here's how you do it in seven steps:

1. Brainstorm for niche site ideas, writing down as many as you can think of. Preferably, these should be in line with what you're passionate about. However, do not cling to a particular idea just because it is a passion of yours. You must be able to be objective and analytical, making doubly sure that your ideas are economically feasible, i.e., popular. Working within a field you are passionate about does have many advantages, though.

2. Once you've generated a pool of ideas, filter or narrow them down using the following set of criteria:

   • Are there many products that you can discuss and review? The number of products you can post about is essential to your niche site taking off. The more products there are in a particular niche, the wider the scope of content you can produce for your visitors.

- Are there good affiliate programs that can provide potentially good commission income for you? Always keep an eye out for opportunities like affiliate programs, in marketing or whatever, these work wonders for many niche websites.

- Are existing niche website marketers actually making money off it? Of course, taking a note of others' experiences is always a great way of improving your game and understanding what to change and what to keep. If you are unsure about taking a certain step along your way, the chances are that someone else has already tried it, so learn from their failure or success.

- Are you able to generate around 100 articles on your niche or topic? Try to think up as many as possible to get an idea of how fruitful the niche you chose really is. If producing around 100 is a struggle, then perhaps your niche is too limited and the idea should be replaced, or at least modified.

1. Set up your website.

2. Begin generating your website's content using this outline:

- Write five review articles, one for each of the five most popular products for your niche;

- Write three very detailed and easy to understand tutorials on your particular market or niche (how-to videos);

- Create three list posts;

- Do it all over again.

1. Join affiliate marketing programs that are related to your market or niche. Individual manufacturers or retailers dealing with products related to your particular niche might want to pay good money to advertise on your website. The chances of getting a serious affiliate marketing deal dramatically increase as your following grows.

2. Research the top 5 to 10 keywords or products to rank for. Use the most popular keywords strategically in your content and you greatly improve your search ranking over time. This is one of the

ways to gradually get closer to the top of the search results.

3. Use Yoast SEO (search engine optimization) specifically for WordPress and perform your niche website SEO for all pages and posts.

4. Email all your friends and social media contacts to spread the word about your niche website. Ask your friends to share it as well and send it further.

5. Sign up for social media accounts for your niche website, e.g., Facebook, Twitter, Instagram and Pinterest. Having pages on such websites will help gather and group up your followers more effectively. You can also use your pages for newsletters, sharing ideas and content, attracting more followers, getting useful feedback, etc. Essentially, social media pages will do for your website what they do for individual people — immensely facilitate communication.

6. Sign up for a HARO (help a reporter out) account. HARO is a service available online that helps journalists obtain feedback, public feedback, allowing them to link up with experts in particular

issues to help them report on topics much better. Since you'll need to generate very good and accurate content like journalists do, a HARO account will be very helpful for you.

7. Identify and list all the major syndicated publications and blogs you'd like to be featured in for good exposure and promotions. Obtaining a spotlight for your niche website in a well-known publication may take you to whole new heights of fame. If that publication is focused closely on the same niche, it's even better because the feature will also be a valuable vouch for your site.

8. Begin to get in touch with blogs and websites in your niche that offer guest story ideas or posts. Other ways to promote and get promoted, such as guest stories, posts, and appearances, are a useful way of cooperation between websites and blogs in the same field.

9. Create a high-quality email series or content that you can give away for free in exchange for people's email addresses. Establishing an email list, through these

and other means, is a handy form of networking as well.

10. Do steps 4 up to 12 again as you continue building links and channels for SEO via social media.

FINDING YOUR NICHE

Earlier, we mentioned that the first thing you'll need to do before even setting up the actual website is to find your niche. Failure to do so may render all your hard work of setting up your site and promoting it useless or wasted because you may end up going for an unprofitable niche.

If you want to find a good niche, you'll need to approach it like writing a blog, where you need to generate a lot of good topics and content. With millions of people in the United States and billions in the world, there is an endless world of niche topics to be discovered and profited from. And, as with Amazon FBA earlier, I highly recommend prioritizing niches that you're very familiar with or are passionate about. Why? Chances are, you're already knowledgeable on it.

Just take note that what I mean by prioritizing is putting it first in terms of studying for profitability and not necessarily going for it. It is certainly possible that what you're passionate and knowledgeable about — say, dung beetles — is not a profitable niche while classic cars — which you may not be passionate about as of the moment — is a profitable one. In which case, go for the classic cars niche. Prioritizing your passions and interest simply means that, given your lack of knowledge on your identified potential niches' profitability, evaluate that of the one you're interested in or are passionate about first.

If you find that your ideal niche is not profitable enough, do not be afraid to go with something that you're not yet knowledgeable about. Take time to read about it and familiarize yourself with it. Once you have enough basic knowledge, you can either research more stuff about it to create enough meaningful content or outsource it to freelance writers. There's more than one way to skin a, well, potato.

The truth is, with the ocean of knowledge that is the Internet, you can become well versed in practically any topic you can think of. Some will take more time to study thoroughly than others, but it can be done nonetheless. Once upon a primitive time, if an individual wanted to become knowledgeable on something, it was either formal education or hundreds, even thousands, of hours in the library. The current state of affairs is such that you can learn and, subsequently, make money off your knowledge from a single place — your chair.

Surely, you can't expect to operate surgically on human brains without formal education and training, but when it comes to information, the Internet is limitless. So, if a niche you want to get involved in lies beyond your expertise, start learning and researching. Think of it as taking a course of sorts in order to get a job.

NARROWING DOWN YOUR LIST OF NICHE IDEAS

When you have laid out all of the prospects and ideas, all that's left is to make the right choice. Now, there are a number of ways to go about this, but it begins with you having a firm understanding of how far your knowledge stretches in certain areas, your capacities to produce content, etc. Having a clear notion of where exactly you want to take your website and what it is that you are hoping to achieve also makes the choice easier.

One of the ways you can filter or short-list your niche ideas is through the margin-volume criteria. Entrepreneurs can be classified as those that prefer selling high-price-low-volume (high-margin) products or low-price-high-volume (low-margin) products. Each has its own advantages and disadvantages. Those with high prices can give you significantly greater profit margins or spreads per unit of sale but, because they're expensive, you'll sell less. In contrast, low-priced products give you significantly less margins and require you to sell more units to generate the same amount of income as selling higher-priced products. Which is better? It is all up to you, depending on the pros and cons of each as it relates to the niche, the products, and the market.

Another filter through which you can narrow down your list of potential niches is the ability to write tons of articles or good content on the niche. A good benchmark — however arbitrary — is 50 to 100 articles. If you see yourself as being able to generate that much content over the course of the year, it means you're interested or passionate about the niche and, as such, are knowledgeable about it. This tells you that you'll probably have enough energy and interest to successfully see this through. If you can't, consider hiring ghostwriters, which of course will cost you more.

Given that hiring freelancers is an expense, you may want to avoid doing so at first. It is probably best to put in the extra effort and produce as much of your own content as possible in the beginning. This way, you will gather the maximum amount of capital, with which you can later hire help. At that point, you will begin to put the operation on autopilot.

Knowing if the niche has affiliate marketing programs that pay good commissions is another key factor to consider when narrowing down your list of niche ideas. While there are affiliate marketing programs for just about anything, what separates the great ones from the laggards are commissions. A good rule of thumb is to go for programs that offer at least 10% commission. Personally, I aim for around 20% to 35% commission. It may be difficult to find and set up the most profitable programs at first, of course, but you should definitely set the bar at 10% at the very least. These standards aren't merely about cashing in as quickly as possible, but also about presenting your website as an ambitious project instead of a cheap, small-time hobby.

Keep in mind that digital products tend to give out higher commissions compared to physical products for one simple reason — cost. Digital products can be easily replicated at very little to no cost at all, while physical products entail costs to reproduce. So, if you're gunning purely for huge commissions, digital products may be best for you. Not to say that physical products suck at commissions. I'm just saying that, while they can pay good commissions, they're not as high as those given to sellers of digital products.

More than just good commissions, you'll also want to find out if a particular niche is one where people actually make money. What good are sky-high commissions on niches with nary a customer? Maybe that's why they're offering high commissions — they're very hard to sell! As is the case with most things in life, if it appears to be too good to be true, then it probably is not—true that is. With all the effort that goes into setting up your site, you do not want to throw it all away in a worthless market!

So how can you know if people actually make money in this niche? Here's how:

First, generate up to 10 keywords that you think people will use in search engines when searching for your product. If it is fat burners, particularly Hydroxycut, people may use the keywords Hydroxycut Hardcore, Hydroxycut Elite, or Hydroxycut reviews, among others.

Next, run these keywords through Market Samurai or Google's Keyword Tool in order to find out just how much traffic these keywords get. More than just discovering how many searches these keywords get monthly, you'll also find other good keywords on your niche or product that you may not have thought of yet.

Now conduct a search on those keywords that generate tons of traffic and notice whether there arc common websites that appear on the first pages of their search results. If there are, check them out. If there are no common ones, simply check out those top-ranking sites per keyword search.

How can you tell if they're making money? Some sites actually divulge that they do, like the website

Kenrockwell.com, wherein he says at the bottom of every page that the website helps him support his family. But most other websites do not do that, so how can you get an idea of whether they're making good money or not?

Market reviews are another way of doing it. If a niche has many product reviews with affiliate links in them, it is a good sign that maybe people are making decent money in the niche. Keep in mind that, while a vibrant market does mean that chances are there's money to be made there, it may also mean fierce competition.

Overall, you can get an idea if people are making money in a particular niche by looking at keyword search traffic, reviews with affiliate links, high-priced products, and high commission rates.

MAKING MONEY THROUGH YOUR NICHE WEBSITE

There are several ways you can actually make money from your niche website, which include direct selling, paid links, paid advertisements, AdSense advertisements, and affiliate marketing. In the next chapter, we'll take a look into the world of affiliate marketing in detail.

On one final note concerning niche websites, although they require significant work to get things up and running smoothly, and entail more risk than with passive income systems in general, they are still at the very top when it comes to passive income potential. Well-established websites that draw in significant amounts of traffic are among the most autonomous passive income endeavors. If a website manages to form a community, it is likely that this community might all but take over most of the functions of the website. Some of the more beloved sites routinely have users gladly assume the roles of administration, sometimes even for free! So if you know what you are doing and set everything up accordingly, this is an opportunity to create an almost living, moneymaking machine.

ADVANCES IN STRATEGIES

A big part of getting noticed is creating something unique or different than what already exists out in the world. Whether you want to create a blog, articles on a specific topic like DIY, products, news, etc., you need to have it "bring something to the table." Why should someone choose to visit your website or read your blog when there are millions of others out there that are similar to yours? You need to find a way to stand out and make a name for yourself, and this can be done by throwing yourself into social media, networking and marketing yourself and your site. Being different means standing out, which in turn means getting noticed.

People have the option to visit different, well-established, and well-reviewed sites – so why should they visit yours? You have to keep asking yourself this and answering the question. If you have something of value that other people will see as valuable and interesting, that needs to be echoed in your site. Make whatever it is you are doing, whether it is original or not, different. For example, maybe you enjoy reviewing movies, so you decide you want to make your own website based on movie critiques. Say you are also very funny and have a knack for adding humorous remarks into your critiques. This could be a great way for your site to get noticed because you are providing a humorous opinion on movies people want to see.

Another example would be selling products. Are you selling something interesting and unique? If so, write an overly wordy, comical description of the products. There are ways to get noticed without using humor; humor is just a good example for the sake of entertainment purposes.

Simon Wolf

Chapter 5
Affiliate Marketing

In the simplest possible terms, affiliate marketing is a passive way of earning income simply by promoting other entrepreneurs' products or services on your web or blog sites. There are many different ways of doing affiliate marketing but, generally speaking, you can earn through commissions — as a percentage of sales — or fixed rates per purchase that product or service providers give you whenever your readers click a link in your web or blog page's content, are directed to the provider's website, and buy the product or service being offered. In other affiliate programs, the visitors who were directed to them by clicking on links on your websites do not have to buy just for you to earn from them — they simply need to take certain actions other than purchasing such as opting in with an email address or completing a survey, among others.

Conversions — or actual sales — are accurately tracked by vendors through a link given to you (the publisher) that contains a code specific to you only, which determines that a given sale came from you. Other vendors may give you a "coupon code" to give away to your readers and this coupon code is what identifies specific sales with you as publisher, which is the basis for paying your commissions.

Affiliate marketing is one of the most — if not the most — preferred media for advertising by many because of cost efficiency. With affiliate marketing, vendors only pay for advertising upon conversion or a particular action as mentioned earlier. Unlike traditional advertising or marketing, vendors do not have to pay for advertisements that fall on deaf ears or, in the case of online marketing, blind eyes. As such, profitability is enhanced.

In other words, affiliate marketing has seen significant growth as opposed to traditional means of advertising because it (usually) offers 100% efficiency on the investment. Paying for billboards, placing television adverts, engaging in sponsorship programs, etc., are often costly and offer no guarantee, whatsoever, that sales will increase. At best, companies can use expert prognosis and consultancy services to improve their marketing tactics in hopes of minimizing risk.

For publishers such as you, affiliate marketing is a winner simply because it gives the opportunity to discover and sell products that are highly relevant to a particular niche of choice, which can give higher income compared to pay-per-click marketing or banner advertising.

On a side note, if your blog, any sort of page, or whatever kind of venture you have got going has amassed a considerable following, it is not a rarity to get offers from vendors who might want to advertise their products to your audiences.

One example of such an offer I know, from personal experience, is of a friend who has had a YouTube channel for a while. A couple of his tutorial videos on a specific subject garnered quite a view count, so one day he was contacted by a company whose business was related to the content of his videos. They actually offered to pay a decent sum of money if he gave them rights to market their products on said videos. This way he cashed in on his content pretty well, and he wasn't even going for it! Imagine what you can accomplish with a mixture of effort, organization, and focus.

OF AFFILIATE MARKETING AND BLOGS

Unlike with niche websites, the relationship between you as a publisher and your readers is much more personal or deeper. Such a relationship enjoys a greater amount of trust and integrity than a niche website. As a result, your blog readers may be more inclined to follow your product or service recommendations than they would a niche website. Now I'm not saying niche websites suck — I mean, I even included it as one of the ways to earn passive income. I'm just saying that for purposes of affiliate marketing, blogging may enjoy a higher conversion rate than niche market websites. The tradeoff, however, is that it takes time for blogging to amass enough loyal followers to be profitable, while niche marketing can give conversions much faster.

Just be careful about the products you promote in your blogs as part of your affiliate marketing campaign. Choose the wrong product and all that hard work you've put into building up your blog's loyal audience can crumble in a moment.

Remember how, back in Chapter 3, I mentioned that one of the greatest benefits of the FBA program is that it allows you to piggyback on the glorious reputation of Amazon? Well, affiliate marketing through your blog is sort of similar, but with you assuming the role of Amazon (on a small scale, of course). Potential partners who want to advertise to your audience are counting precisely on the reputation you enjoy among your dedicated readers.

Vendors are fully aware that the average person doesn't care much for ads, especially while they are spending their leisure time cruising through the Internet. Well, a consumer is much more likely to check their advert out if it comes from a trusted source, such as their favorite blogger. This is especially true if the blogger directly recommends or endorses the product. Now, with all that trust on your mind, imagine what would become of your blog if you misused that trust to advertise a substandard product? Oh, boy.

GETTING STARTED WITH AFFILIATE MARKETING

Yes, affiliate marketing can be really lucrative but it is not picking money off trees, mind you. While many people do earn money from affiliate marketing, only a few get to earn a fortune because affiliate marketing success is highly dependent on several factors such as website traffic, product relevance, product quality, trust between publisher and readers, willingness of readers to buy, and ability to write great sales copy. And, speaking of willingness to buy, you'll have to be careful to ensure that you do not push your readers too hard or sell low-quality products because it won't just ruin your chances of converting them to paying customers for your vendors, you also risk ruining your brand or personal reputation, the latter being especially true if you do affiliate marketing through your own blog instead of a niche website.

There are plenty of articles on the Internet warning bloggers about the risks of affiliate marketing and stories about misguided advertising campaigns that have ruined successful bloggers' careers. Have you ever stopped following or unsubscribed from a content creator simply because of the onslaught of adverts, especially bad ones, that irreversibly changed their platform for the worse? Haven't you at least considered it from time to time? I know I have, and then some!

No matter how loyal a following you might have, they can only be pushed so far before your platform begins to crumble like a house of cards. So exercise extreme caution and never forget your integrity; your audience may care about it even more than you do.

So how can you actually make money from affiliate marketing?

Business Model

Basically, there are two models you can choose from: resource and review sites. Your choice of business model depends on how familiar you are with the product or service you'll advertise.

On a resource website, a merchant partner's (vendor) website is embedded in affiliate links that are included in your website's contents, e.g., posts and articles. The resource site model needs regular updates and relatively fresh content to keep customers coming back to your website. So, if you're going at it on your own, it will require some work, especially if the site's sole purpose is to draw ad revenue. As always, the writing can be allocated to others for a higher degree of passivity in your income. This form of advertising is among the most passive in and of itself, though; or, rather, it is very tame. Usually, it comes as links on the sidelines of your content posts. So you can imagine that this is the form of advertising your readers are least likely to be annoyed by, as it just sits there waiting to be clicked on by those who are interested. This is precisely why it is so important to attract traffic from people who are most likely to want to buy these products, and it is why you must go out of your way to ensure that the products have value and are related to your niche. Being random or leaving anything to chance in this racket is a sure way to failure.

On the other hand, review websites feature — as the name suggests — product or service reviews of products or services you have personally used or availed yourself of. Each of those review articles features links or banner advertisements that — when clicked by your readers — will direct them to your partner merchant's website. One advantage to this kind of business model is that it doesn't need frequent updates or regular new materials. As a marketer or publisher, all you need to do is make minor tweaks on your site to let search engines count you in their search results for relevant keywords.

Now, there are various kinds of partnership programs when it comes to review websites. In particular, one successful form of advertising through reviews is an agreement between you and the manufacturer wherein he supplies you with new products for you to test and review them. There are many such examples easily found throughout the Internet. These gigs do not necessarily have to go through a website either, as many successful tech blogs, YouTube channels, etc., have formed such relationships with companies, sometimes not just any companies, but some of the biggest names in the business. The founders of these pages and websites make quite a prosperous living this way.

Again, it is all about amassing a sizeable following first, so this system may not be within your reach at the very start, but is definitely something to consider as a long-term goal.

Website

To be an affiliate marketer, you need your very own platform from which to advertise stuff, either a website or a blog. If you do not have a site or blog, you'll need to create one or the other. This is where a lot of the necessary work is involved, but it is also important to fully understand the difference between these two platforms before you get to it. Consider the following advantages and shortcomings, and see what fits best with the kind of dedication and approach you plan.

The main advantage of hosting a blog as a means of promoting your merchant partners' products is that you can do so for free, with platforms such as WordPress or Blogger. On the other hand, you'll need to pay certain fees, however minimal, to set up a new website. You'll also need to design or hire someone to do so for you if you choose to set up a website while the blog sites I mentioned provide templates, both free and paid, so you do not have to worry about having to design your website.

When starting out, getting a site where it can be hosted for free is one of the best ways to go, especially if you are highly inexperienced. These sites, such as WordPress, can be highly adaptable should you decide to merge a different domain name or decide to host your own site. It can be really easy to transfer the blog or website, but if you can't do it yourself, you can employ someone for a small fee to do it for you via platforms like Upwork or Fiverr. There is a large amount of potential in sites like WordPress because you can manipulate the site to make it your own. There is also a variety of templates available that can be easily installed, adding more personality to your website.

If you want a more professional sounding blog site, simply buy a domain name and link it with your blog site — usually for a fee — or you can directly pay for such on your blog site. Between the two, http://passiveincome.com sounds more professional than http://passiveincome.wordpress.com, right? Although it may seem silly to some, little things like this do matter, as they showcase a certain level of dedication and even reliability. It is never a waste of time and money (within reasonable limits, of course) to try to improve your image, especially when you are trying to make a name for yourself and expand. This is true for basically all business ventures.

Pick a Niche

Before you even choose your products or services to promote, you'll need to figure out your niche or specialization area. While it is certainly ideal to pick a niche that you're already knowledgeable about, you shouldn't be limited by it. You can also consider niches that you're merely interested in or are enthusiastic in learning more about. Because the initial work of starting up can be very thorough, it is important to pick a niche that you're interested in so you won't mind the relatively long hours required to set it up at the beginning. You can use the same guidelines listed in the chapter on niche website marketing to pick a good niche for affiliate marketing.

It is significantly easier to pick something that you are interested in or knowledgeable about: It will relieve you of a significant amount of work and stress, since you won't have to do as much research on the topic and it won't feel as if you are grasping to stay focused due to disinterest. Writing alone can be difficult and getting started is the most difficult part. Choosing your topics wisely and by area of interest can be a huge advantage.

This can be a purely strategic choice if you want it to be, as well. Some people are able to disregard their own areas of interest and their passions completely; they instead focus solely on the income potential of the niche they are choosing. These individuals can adapt and prosper in virtually any field. You do not have to be one of those people just to make the right choice, but the truth is that this kind of attitude is an automatic advantage in the business of making money. A wise consideration of pros and cons and a compromising approach to choosing your niche will do just fine, though.

Pick the Product or Service

After picking the niche you'd like to specialize in, it is time to choose the products or services you'd like to promote on your chosen platform. The nature of your chosen niche will determine, to a great extent, the products and services you'll promote and the amount of work you'll need to put in.

Some niches may be profitable, but they might also be very limiting, in the sense that they do not offer much room for you to maneuver. What I mean by this is that certain niches are too specific, and thus do not provide a wide range of topics. Always consider the amount of material in your chosen area. It could be a good idea to go with niches that are very general, but also enjoy an immense amount of interest, like tech, for example. This is a niche with possibly the widest spectrum of topics and products today and, not only that, but it is constantly in the public focus.

For more traditional products and services, go with companies like Commission Junction, while, if you'd like to focus more on digital products, an alternative like ClickBank or PayDotCom is the way to go. You can find details on how to join them on their websites. On these websites, you can find many partner merchants to work with for your niche and platform.

It is also a good idea to make sure that you do not start with a wide range of products or options. You need to start with a few products with a good, solid selection. If you bring in too many products or too many options at once, you risk not selling certain items and losing a bunch of money because you have items that won't sell. If you choose, say, woman's underwear, start with a few different styles in several colors that you know are popular (black, white, nude, pink, red) and see which of the styles are most popular, phasing out the less popular items.

Then, as time goes on, bring in new products and see how well those sell and how popular those become, again phasing out the less popular items. By doing this, you will build a solid product line that you know people love and you know people will buy, lessening the chance that you will have a large amount of product that you are unable to sell.

Direct Traffic

After you've chosen your product or service, it is time to get prospects to visit your affiliate program. How do you do this? There's a multitude of ways to go about this and they usually entail various forms of networking or simply producing content. But whatever needs doing will have to be done, because traffic is the alpha and omega of affiliate marketing. This is true of some kinds of affiliations more than others but, as traffic increases, so will your income.

Probably the easiest and highly successful way of doing this is posting web articles or blogs and — if you already have an email list — use your email newsletters to entice those in your email list to get on your affiliate marketing program. As always, be mindful not to end up spamming people, as they'll quickly block you and politely show your emails their way into the junk folder. It is all about balance and optimization if you are to keep everyone happy, including your bank. Science is still to determine whether those old-school pestering adverts we encounter in our daily lives are worse than spam, but the odds are about 80% in spam's favor so far.

You can also drive traffic to your program by giving away free but quality content like free reports or ebooks about your particular niche that can help drive a significant amount of traffic to your affiliate links. People just love free stuff, especially if it is related to the things they're interested in or are passionate about. Amazon's Audible Company is a great example of this tactic being effectively implemented, by giving away free audio books to draw in more customers, and it works great. Note, however, that one reason it works so well is the sheer awesomeness. It is not hard to make people want to buy more of the product they just got for free if the product is great. Better yet, potential customers get to choose which particular audio book they want to download!

Providing free products to your audience can also be an efficient means of acquiring emails for your list. Coupons or even discounts, as well as the products I already mentioned, all can be offered in exchange for a person's email. This is 10 seconds of your reader's time, so you both benefit. We'll get deeper into this later on.

DEVELOPING YOUR AFFILIATE MARKETING PROGRAM

Now that you've successfully set up your affiliate marketing program, it is time to make it grow and earn more income. Here are a couple of ways you can do that.

Watch and Learn

You can quickly and easily grow as an affiliate marketer by learning from others who have already succeeded at it. If you do not personally know any experienced affiliate marketer, have no fear. There are many online forums and communities you can join for free, from which you can learn a lot of things about growing your business. You can also often learn about valuable resources from such groups for free. Some of the best groups to join are Warrior Forum, ABestWeb and Digital Point. More than just resources and advice, you get opportunities to establish connections with other affiliate marketers. How cool is that, huh?

The opposite side of the learning coin, studying the ways and reasons that others failed, is equally important. Success comes through a mixture of two inseparable pillars of wisdom — knowing what to do and what not to do. So, while you are taking insights from successful affiliate marketers, look up the stories of failure as well. I'm not going to scare you and say that there are plenty, because there probably aren't, but there are surely a few, and you need to learn as much as you can from them.

Talking to others and asking questions is the only way to learn, aside from diving in yourself. It is highly beneficial to learn how others made it and how others didn't, using the same or different techniques. Each person succeeds differently because each person is different, so going online and finding other people who are like you may give you a good idea at how well you can succeed...maybe not, but isn't it worth a shot? You need to do anything you can do to give yourself an edge in the business. Take all the knowledge you can get and then take some more. There is an endless amount of knowledge out there to learn from individuals who are, or were, in the same boat as you are, and they are more than willing to help you.

Believe it or not, the tales of other people's failure are even motivational at times, depending on how you look at it. Either way, you must be armed with information and know the experience of both sides of the spectrum if you want to maximize your chances of triumph.

Establish Relationships

Speaking of connections, relationships are key to any successful affiliate marketing program. While passive in nature, you'll need to put in a great amount of work and patience before you start making significant money from affiliate marketing. While your affiliate marketing program drives the necessary traffic to your website, you are responsible for creating strong relationships with your merchant partners, which is key to getting favorable terms and conditions. You'll also need to continue developing relationships with other merchant partners in order to diversify your products and services, which is another key to continuously enjoying good affiliate marketing success and profits.

As your affiliate marketing business continues to grow, the deals, commissions, and various other perks will continue to improve and bring in more income. Keep maintaining and consolidating your relationships and partnerships; you never know what new opportunities could arise and take your endeavor even further.

This includes all, and I really do mean all, correspondence and communications to partners being done with the highest amount of respect and professionalism. Your emails need to be drafted in a professional manner because they are a reflection of your Internet presence and should be conducted as such. Regardless of emotions, every disagreement also needs to be handled with respect and patience. Keeping a level head under stress shows potential customers that you know how to do business and you know how to be a leader, which are hard qualities to come by. Big merchants know other big merchants so, if one merchant was highly satisfied working with you, they may refer you to someone else, building more relationships and generating more potential passive income for you in the future.

Targeted Traffic

More than just directing people to your blog or website, you'll need to direct the right kinds of people to them. Who are they? They're people who may be considered potential customers — people who are interested enough to consider clicking on your merchant partners' links on your site — and may actually buy the product or service offered.

All the traffic or clicks in the world won't amount to much if you do not attract a specific group of people, who are likely to be interested and ultimately buy the marketed products. Once this train starts rolling the way it should, your commissions will do the rest.

There are four ways to attract prospects or sales leads:

1. Paid Advertising: You'll need to use a highly clickable link, graphics, and ad copy. Compared to regular or traditional affiliate marketing programs, this way of attracting prospects (normally using pay-per-click-ads) allows you to earn money even if the prospect doesn't buy the product or service. Suffice it to say

that this system will be profitable if your platform enjoys copious amounts of traffic, but may prove inefficient with smaller bases. If your particular website or blog is not quite there yet, it may be better to go after hard commissions at first.

2. Free Advertising: You can do this through advertisements and links on websites that are generally free, such as US Free Ads and Craigslist. You and the website earn money whenever someone clicks on your advertisement or link. Although it is not the most lucrative solution, it should be a great way to get started and grow your business stronger.

3. Article Marketing: The primary way this method works is by aiming for a higher ranking in search engine queries for particular keywords through establishing the marketer as a source that's highly credible and one who won't utilize software to spam customers. Websites such as Ezine Articles allow affiliate marketers like you to publish articles that feature a "resource box" that's unique to you. When other website managers and bloggers share or republish your articles together with the intact

resource box, your search engine ranking gradually climbs.

4. Email Marketing: Here you can embed an option for subscribing to email newsletters, updates, and what-have-yous for your website's visitors. Doing this can help you build up your email list, which will be useful for your affiliate marketing and email marketing campaigns. Later, in a designated chapter, you will see why it is important to take every chance you get and use every available tool to build your email list more easily.

Quality over Quantity

While it is good for your affiliate marketing business to have a diversified list of merchant partners, overdoing it can be counterproductive. For one, more doesn't necessarily mean merrier — in terms of income, at least. Experts agree that the real key to successfully pulling off an affiliate marketing campaign is picking the right niche and the best merchant partners, i.e., the right products and services. If you've got those down pat, it doesn't matter if you only have one or two merchant partners.

More partners, and thus more ads, can also be detrimental because people do not want to be buried in ads, plain and simple. Your audience will not mind an optimized and evened-out number of adverts coming their way, and they will take the time to give them a look, but do not take it too far. It wouldn't be a bad idea to apply an adaptation of the Golden Rule here: Put yourself in their shoes and consider how many ads you would be willing to tolerate on the websites and blogs that you frequent. A few successful and well-paying partners will do the trick just fine, leaving all the parties satisfied and, most important, your readers will not be annoyed and will keep coming back.

ADVANCES IN STRATEGIES

While it may seem obvious, choosing the right products to advertise will make or break your business. In order to pick the right products, it would be wise to try out some of the products you wish to advertise to verify their reliability and quality. If you praise a product for its durability without ever trying it and your customers purchase the product only to find out it is cheaply made and falls apart, it will not only cut down on future product purchases but will also lower your credibility.

Owning a blog or website that has followers and regular readers is almost like having a group of friends. One of your friends has great DIY ideas, so everyone looks to her for DIY advice and projects. Keeping your reliability and credibility can be among the only things keeping you afloat in a market as saturated as the blogging industry. Every day people are getting burned out on blogging and new people are becoming interested.

Who's to say your blog doesn't have the potential to get picked up and noticed – which is why maintaining a solid foundation based on trust and reliability through your readers and audience is so important. Know the products that are advertised on your site, because remaining ignorant can cause significantly more issues in the long run.

Simon Wolf

Chapter 6
Email Marketing

As the name suggests, this is a way of earning passive income by using email to sell your products and services to people. To successfully earn passive income through email marketing, you need an email list, which is a list of people who subscribed to your regular email distribution system, typically newsletters that provide them with useful or interesting content.

There are two kinds of email lists: discussion and announcement. In discussion lists, all the members in the list have access to all the other members, i.e., they can send emails to them. In announcement lists, only you as administrator or list owner can do that. In most cases, announcement lists are primarily used for sending regular email newsletters and announcements, while discussion lists are primarily for creating virtual communities where people who are interested in a particular niche or topic can discuss it together.

This interaction between subscribers within your discussion email list has some underlying benefits that you can make good use of: Namely, an interconnected and decentralized community that will always be able to share and expand more effectively. If you want to create a more vibrant community, this is the way to go. Announcement email lists are more suitable for an already well-established community of subscribers, these being regular customers or followers of your brand.

HOW TO BUILD YOUR EMAIL LIST

There are two ways to acquire your own email list —build it yourself or buy it. For efficient and meaningful advertising, taking the time and putting in the effort to establish your own list definitely has quite a few advantages over the alternative. Why build an email list? There are several reasons. For one, if you are going to stick to the virtual, self-employed, passive income business, you are going to need a web page of your own. If you intend to write eBooks and sell products on Amazon, you will need a home base. With this home base, your email list, you can spread the word on new products and books via your email list; even offering customers and your audience samples of your products or discount codes.

As you continue to build your list of email subscribers, you will always have a way to reach out to your following and ask for opinions or ask them to check out something new you have done. You can also use this as a way to advertise other people's products through affiliate marketing, but we will get into that later. We'll discuss both options in more detail. Let's first talk about building it up.

Landing Pages

The fastest way to build your email list is by directing quality traffic to your product or service's landing page; and, by "quality," I mean people who are prospects, not mere kibitzers or curious cats.

One of the best places to start is — surprise — Facebook! This is because advertising on Facebook allows you to target your desired market, i.e., the right demographics. In particular, you can choose your advertisements' target audiences based on age, gender, location, interests, and even the status of their relationships, among others. This is an important advantage because the more accurate or focused your advertising is, the more potent it becomes. Due to the extensive detail of personal information that Facebook is given by its users, it has long become a website with limitless marketing potential. Many companies, from smaller to gigantic ones, know full well of this convenience, which is why they often dedicate sizeable amounts of money to Facebook's ad programs. If I didn't know any better, I'd say that this is actually one of the most relevant factors contributing to Facebook's enormous net worth.

If nothing else, Facebook provides businesses a way to communicate and respond directly to their customers and audience, giving your business or web page a personality. Nowadays, people do not want to speak to automated services and they do not want to post something to a business's Facebook page if they won't get a response. You can use Facebook as a direct communication line from your web page to your Facebook, and vice versa.

Keeping your page up to date is just as important as updating your website. You need to always stay active so that you are constantly appearing in your followers' news feeds and constantly driving traffic. As you show up in their news feeds and they react to your posts or comment on your page, this shows up on their friend's news feeds also, and so on, reaching millions of individuals. This is why Facebook is such a fantastic landing page.

You can also build up your email list by putting up landing pages that are specifically dedicated to giving away free resources and have sign-up forms (where they can leave their email addresses in exchange for the freebies) that are very easy to see. And, speaking of landing pages, good ones do not have distracting elements and are focused only on getting people's email addresses in exchange for free resources like reports, ebooks and other downloadable stuff. Many sites function solely with this purpose, offering discounts, shopping coupons, or niche products, digital or physical. The mere fact that these sites exist shows just how profitable this form of advertising can be.

Discount Codes

You can get email addresses to build up your list by using a pop-up window that offers your website's visitors the opportunity to get discount codes in return for their email addresses. In particular, this works well with people who are already familiar with the products and services you're planning to promote or are already promoting via email. Even though they are often annoying to most, pop-ups can be more than welcome if they bring with them those discounts or any free stuff. Basically, you can hardly ever go wrong with giveaways.

Just keep in mind that, while many people sign up for the discounts, they normally take their sweet time in using them, so do not get discouraged if this doesn't boost your sales right away. The key here is building relationships by consistently giving them free but quality content through email. Of course, if your sales are still stagnating after a considerable amount of time has passed, it might be time to alter or modify your program in some way, especially if you are sending out a lot of discounts and free products. Although building a genuine relationship with your customers is important, you do not want to be taken advantage of and go bankrupt by giving too many discount codes without any actual result.

Speaking of discount codes, you can easily make these through an app called JustUno, which gives out free plans that you can utilize for giving away discount codes to prospects in exchange for their email addresses. Just make your own discount code, plug it into the app, and customize how you'd like it to look on a widget.

Facebook Contests and Giveaways

Another good way to build up both your email list and social media following is by giving away your products, services, or other cool stuff for free on your brand's Facebook page. People can join simply by liking your business' Facebook page and giving their email addresses — that's it. You hit two birds with one stone — more email addresses and Facebook followers.

One way to maximize your chance of successfully acquiring email addresses and social media followers with this method is by making sure that you use a very good quality picture of the product you're planning to give away so you can easily grab people's attention, even if their newsfeed sections are already clogged and busy. Such pictures can also make your contest posts easier to share.

Another way to attract even more followers to your Facebook page through contests is simply by introducing some additional beneficial rules. For example, set it up to ask people not to only like your page, but also to share the post announcing the contest with their friends, preferably via their own wall. Of course, be careful that you do not push it too far; consider your particular product and the potential interest it might spark, if any. If your brand or page is very specific and has a dedicated following already interested in your product, then it would be much easier to convince them to share. Otherwise, do not force it; if you are introducing a new or unrelated product, chances are they won't want to share any such thing with their friends.

These contests can be fun for everyone, even the business owner. There are many different ways to advertise on media and using social media platforms is highly enjoyable. For example, we all remember the "Ice Bucket Challenge" and how that helped to raise awareness for a certain cause by someone dumping ice water over their head and then tagging more people to do the same. This challenge reached millions of people, raising awareness and money for the cause. Your business may not be able to reach that many people with a challenge of that magnitude, but you can incorporate public participation, aside from just having them share and like your page.

For example, if you are a theme park, you can have people post pictures in a funniest theme park selfies contest and have the Facebook audience vote on the funniest picture. If you are a local restaurant, you can talk about the great city you live in and ask people to post pictures of the city along with liking and sharing your page; in return they will receive a coupon of some sort. Any way in which you can reach out and have the public participate in advertising your business with you, you have the potential to reach many more people than if you were to attempt to do it on your own.

If you need help in creating Facebook contests and giveaways, you can use the Rafflecopter and Woobox apps. They're free and easy to use.

Sign-Up Boxes

The old-fashioned way of putting a sign-up box for opting in with email addresses on your website still works well in these relatively modern times. However, this one is particularly useful when you already have a blog that regularly features high-quality content. It is because regular content can make people want to sign up in your email list on their own so they can get more of it in the future; i.e., no cajoling or calls to action needed. It is like good coffee — you can never get enough of it.

This simple principle — convenience — happens to still work just fine. If your platform has daily or weekly content, your dedicated readers will much prefer to be notified directly via email than to have to come back regularly to check for new publications. So, if you are a content creator of this sort, you're in luck because you can basically build your email list by simply making your blog or site more accessible to your audience. An epitome of win-win, do not you think?

BUYING EMAIL LISTS

Buying email lists is perfectly legal and can really make it much, much easier for you because — I'll be honest — building up an email list requires a lot of hard work, consistency, creativity, and time. It is this appeal that makes buying email lists so popular these days.

So should you buy email lists and save much time and effort to speed things up?

No. Nada. Never. The popularity of this practice is entirely undeserved. This is yet another example where that good old saying about easy streets comes into play — there is no such thing as an easy street.

Why? First off, you do not want email addresses for the sake of having email addresses. What you want are good email addresses, i.e., those that belong to good prospects for selling your stuff to. Obviously, the only way your email list can be useful to the advertising in your particular trade is if you built it in the first place. The only way to guarantee that you have a quality list is by constructing it yourself around your specific business. The interests of the people on the list must pertain to what you are selling. And, simply put, email lists that are for sale aren't good quality at all.

Keep in mind, a lot of people have more than one email address. Some people have three or four or even more email addresses; some are specifically dedicated to using for spam and ads. This way, when they are browsing the Internet, if the option comes up for them to give their email address in order to access a site or access an ad, the email they give has a high likelihood of being one of the email addresses they never use. So, while the email addresses you purchase may have thousands of email addresses, 90% of those email addresses are probably not used, and the remaining 10% aren't interested and will probably become angry when they see an email that they didn't sign up for in their inbox.

Think of it this way. If you have a very good list of email addresses that are actually converting or buying from you, will you share it with others even if they pay you for it? I doubt you will — they might even poach your best accounts from you! Now do you see why it makes sense to say that most email lists are practically crap?

Another reason to stay away from buying email lists is that the people who own those lists hardly know you, if at all. If they do not know you, why would they consider going to your website? Further, why should they even choose to continue receiving email from you? They'll just remove themselves from your list or redirect your emails to the trash bin automatically. And that, my friend, is a waste of money. Not to mention, it can damage your reputation as an email marketer. More harm than benefit.

Oh, I'm not done yet. Another reason to avoid buying lists like the plague is because the reputation of your IP address (think of it as your Internet marketing id) can be compromised. Without going into too many technical details, sending emails to addresses in an email list you acquired through purchasing runs the risk of your IP address being tagged and reported to anti-spamming authorities as spam. When this happens, you might as well say goodbye to your email marketing campaigns. Remember — spamming is diabolical! Well, at least in the world of online marketing, and particularly from the perspective of customers.

As you can see, it is better to build up your email list with good old hard work and creativity rather than shortcutting your email marketing campaigns to the garbage bin. Avoiding this fruitless investment should really be a no-brainer for anybody wielding, at least, a modicum of common sense, let alone someone who is on his way to online marketing success — you, my dear reader, of course.

Thou shalt not buy — email lists, that is!

HOW MARKET VIA EMAIL

While email marketing looks pretty simple and easy to do, it is not just a simple matter of sending random emails that sell your stuff to people on your email list. No, you'll have to be much cleverer and craftier than that! Moreover, that list will have to consist of high-potential subscribers your business can benefit from. You should refrain from sending as much marketing email as possible; instead, opt to send out fewer but higher-quality emails to avoid spamming people. Some people consider two emails a month to be spam whereas others do not consider it spam unless it hits their inbox multiple times in a week; it depends on the person. You need to market with tasteful graphics and catch phrases using a minimum number of emails in an attempt to make the same impact.

There is no point in sending marketing emails to people who just aren't interested. That would be the equivalent of putting up a billboard on the side of a desolate dirt road in the Sahara Desert, advertising an electrical heat radiator. Not too bright! Here are the ways you can wisely use email to earn income via sales.

Newsletters

Sending regular newsletters is one fine way to maintain a current and active email list. Just be careful not to come across as an aggressive salesperson or you'll just drive them away. Strangely enough, considering the subject of this book, I have to say that you shouldn't be too passive either. Advertising is cleverness, creativity, strategy, and planning but, most important, it is persistence. You have to engage your wits and your focus if you are to strike a chord with your customers. Advertising can sometimes really be boiled down to an art, which is one of the reasons that the industry has become so highly competitive.

Make your newsletters about current, up-to-date, relevant, and quality content from other sources as well as your own material. Consistently sending such newsletters can help you build a solid reputation as an expert or authority in your niche, which can foster good relationships that will eventually translate into sales.

And, by regularly providing high-quality content, you subtly ingrain in them the habit of checking emails that you send instead of just going past them in their inboxes or, worse, deleting them without even reading.

However, some individuals become annoyed with receiving regular emails from certain companies. If would be wise to send out a mass email asking who would like to be a part of the list and who wouldn't; anyone who doesn't answer will automatically be added to the list or vice versa. Newsletters are a great way to provide regular emails and information on what is going on with an organization or a business, but a lot of time they aren't the interest of your audience or customers unless there is an incentive in it for them such as discounted products, coupons or free items.

Let It Drip

I'm not talking about coffee here. I'm talking about sending drip email sequences, which is a fancy, technical term used to describe the process of automatically sending a scheduled series of emails with high-quality content to your new email list subscribers. This is done with the use of an autoresponder, which is software that sends a series of scheduled emails to people, particularly your newest subscribers. This way, you can just sit pretty and your computer — via an autoresponder — will take care of the nitty-gritty of sending an accurate and prompt series of high-quality content. All you need to do is create the quality content, divide the content to create a series, and program your autoresponder to deliver each of the emails in the series automatically.

It is very easy and convenient to create your own autoresponders by availing yourself of the services of reputable companies like MailChimp and Aweber. If you're looking for one that specializes in drip sequencing, consider the service called Drip.

Now, there is one important thing should be noted about adapting your content into a serial gig: When you're chopping up content and shaping it up to become a series, do not overdo it! If you spread it out too thin, it may become obvious and emit a vibe of laziness. Be objective and ask yourself twice if you have enough content for a series, and put in a little more work if you do not. Trust me, it will pay off. Granted, it is called drip emailing, but people still do not like to be fed content by the drop. Nonetheless, if you are responsible and clever in the way you do things, the content can still be stretched out pretty far with great success.

Seasonal Promos

One of the traditional ways of marketing through email is by sending emails and notifications to subscribers based on holidays or seasons that are approaching. It is not uncommon for email marketers to email their subscribers about summer, Christmas, Thanksgiving and Black Friday promotions, among others. You can, if you choose, make it even more personal by sending an email birthday greeting to your subscribers with a nice gift like a free resource or a discount code, which can prompt them to buy your stuff.

If you happen to be marketing specific products, it would be a clever move to theme the products themselves according to the season, if possible. Emails spirited in the vibe of seasons and holidays are great, but special offers and unique products are even better. Consider the market and even the psychology and the mood of the customers; some things are incomparably easier to sell during Christmas, for example, whether it is for practical or emotional reasons.

Keep in mind that regular seasonal promotions will make your customers more inclined to wait until specific seasons and holidays to purchase because they know it is going to go on sale. This usually is not a problem for larger companies with a variety of products, but for smaller companies with a small number of products, especially products that are more specialized and expensive, knowing that a large discount is right around the corner could cause them to hold off until they can get the item for a price that they feel is better.

Exclusive Promos and Discounts

You can include special promos and discount codes in your messages to your email subscribers whenever you send out regular newsletters, an autoresponder series, or promo emails. This may just be the slight push they need to buy your product or more of it!

You can actually personalize your discount codes, making unique ones for each person in your email list. However, this can be too much to handle for you or any email marketer. It is better if you use just one, multiple-use discount code for all your subscribers instead. Just make sure that the code has a limited validity period and inform your subscribers accordingly.

By limiting the discount code's validity period, you achieve two things. First, you prevent them from using the code several times, even in the far future as some might feel like doing. Secondly, having a deadline helps create a sense of urgency to use them, which of course translates to sales for your online passive income business. Your customers won't mind that the discounts are time-sensitive either. The sense of urgency is becoming pretty much the norm in today's world and, coupled with the fact that people just like buying things, it has become completely routine for discount codes to have an expiration date.

Be careful to make sure you do not offer discounts and promos too frequently, because customers will wait to buy products until they are on sale if they know they go on sale frequently. This is especially true of anything regular like seasonal promotions or weekly/monthly sales. People are more inclined to wait to purchase knowing they are getting a better price, meaning less money in your pocket after all is said and done. Offering sporadic and random discounts and promos, or only offering them in exclusive newsletters, is a great way to keep your customer base on their feet while still having items purchased at full price.

Social Media Promo Notifications

You can use your email list to build your social media presence. Simply notify your email list subscribers of your ongoing Facebook giveaways or contests and let them know that they can join and have a chance for cool stuff simply by "liking" or "following" your product on Facebook.

This is a means of tying up loose ends, if you will, by getting as many of your followers as possible to be present on all of your platforms, from your email list to any and all pages you have set up across the web. As a useful form of networking, it is a good idea to try consolidating your business this way to strengthen your brand.

ADVANCES IN STRATEGIES

As with everything nowadays, you should make sure that what you are offering to your email list is of value. Valuable knowledge, valuable products; you want to give people a reason to sign up and stay continuous readers. This is a difficult field to get into because people rarely read newsletters that come in their email. They may browse them quickly for free products or coupons, but it is rare that everyone reads an entire newsletter. This doesn't mean that you can be lax about any of the content and offerings in your newsletters; they need to be quality, error-free works every time.

Taking a look at email: How many newsletters have you signed up for? Most people have a few that regularly arrive in their inboxes. How many of these do you read whenever they arrive? While reading, how many do you follow outside ads too? I am not asking these questions to deter you, by any means, only to give you a good idea of the volume of readers you need to make any kind of decent money. Even a couple of hundred dedicated readers may not be enough to generate enough income to make producing the newsletter worthwhile. Newsletters can take a lot of time to develop and obtain quality content for and, because of this, people tend to steer away from creating on a whim. If you have an established business, however, a newsletter is a great way to keep in contact with the past, present, and future customers or clients.

Chapter 7
Udemy (Online Courses)

Online learning continues to increase in popularity and Udemy is one of the major platforms for it. There is a very valid reason. Whether to supplement one's formal education or to compensate for the lack thereof, this form of learning is becoming less and less limited every week. It is, therefore, no surprise that the platforms that offer education have become a profitable business, with the potential to even become educational authorities on an institutional level in the future.

As is the case with all of the business centers on the Internet, Udemy also presents many opportunities for clever and ambitious folks like you. Due to the broad spectrum of learning levels, from entry level to highly advanced, it is a great platform on which to get started if you want to, and are able to, create online courses. It doesn't matter much if you happen to be less than an expert in the chosen field; virtually anybody can set up an online course here. The users are the ones who will judge if your course is adequate or not — reflecting it in your income or feedback. Of course, this means that if you do, in fact, lack knowledge on an individual subject, you should take the time to research and get well versed in the area before you try to teach others about it.

Unlike massive open online courses (MOOC), which are primarily geared toward collegiate subjects, Udemy gives experts from all walks of life a platform in which to create their own courses that they can offer to the general public either for free or for a fee. Further, Udemy gives people the necessary tools to create their own courses, market them, and earn income from them.

Unfortunately, Udemy courses aren't credentialed for college credit as of now. That shouldn't be a problem because Udemy's market is made up of people who want to take courses that are geared toward learning or improving on practical, job-related skills and not getting higher grades. Some courses however, are inclined toward earning credits for specific technical certifications.

As of the start of 2016, Udemy has reportedly served more than 10 million people with over 40,000 courses. At that rate, this platform will certainly find itself right at the top of this market very soon. This is why the time is ripe for you to get on board with this program and find a place for your passive income plans on Udemy. Even if you are an actual expert on your topic, teaching often goes both ways so, in the process of providing these courses to others, you may very well become more proficient and expand your own knowledge at the same time! We'll take a closer look at this potential and a few important things to note as you embark on this venture.

BEFORE YOU CREATE A COURSE ON UDEMY...

Do not rush it. The very purpose of a course dictates that you be meticulous and thorough. Learning can sometimes be hard for many people, and it will be your job on Udemy to make sure that you deliver a comprehensive, well-structured and highly effective course. Hey, you may even reflect on your school days while you're at it, and find that your teachers had it worse than you ever imagined! Before you start creating your course for upload to Udemy, consider reflecting on the following.

Potential Income

While top Udemy instructors make a fortune in Udemy, not everyone earns a big income. It is worth noting that some instructors only bring in $60 monthly but the elite ones earn six figures annually. Do not let this discourage you, as this doesn't necessarily mean a lot of competition for you in particular, nor does it mean that the top is occupied. If anything, it simply goes to show how far you can go through this website. If a course creator is not pulling in a significant amount of income, this is probably because they either haven't produced quality or have chosen to teach an unpopular or perhaps too popular skill. On the other hand, those who are drawing six figures have probably worked very, very hard for their position and have reached a level of organization and proficiency that can't be expected of a beginner. Obviously, at that level they are probably some kind of a company or, at least, a team of instructors, so no need to compare yourself to these circles on Udemy yet!

Either way, you shouldn't feel too strongly about either of these extremes. With focus, creativity, and due diligence you can get to exactly where you want to be.

Time Frame

Making an online course will require a lot of investment from you, particularly in terms of time, and possibly resources. For some people, especially book authors, it takes as much time as writing a full-fledged book. Obviously, it is much easier if you already have a book or some other original material like blogs and workshops on which you can base your course. You can probably create a course in a two- to three-hour sitting with such materials available. But if you're practically starting from scratch, allot a lot of time for it and budget that time wisely.

Even if you have the ability to create the course within a two- to four-hour time frame, you should refrain from doing so for multiple reasons. There is a reason that you should take your time. When you rush into things, you make mistakes and ideas begin to become blurred. Same thing with driving: You do not drive at high rates of speed because you would lose control and the same goes for ideas. Slow down and draw out an outline one night, maybe even two nights. Slowly ease into the project and figure out the message you want to send. Going too fast leaves too much room to omit important information that could be crucial in learning the topic you are trying to teach. You do not want to make any mistakes to hurt your credibility as a teacher and therefore you should only create courses with the utmost quality, creativity, and enthusiasm.

Now, what you are providing is a course, yes, but this doesn't mean that there can't be some kind of a pitch attached to it. As a matter of fact, it could potentially do wonders for your project. If you go back to school for a moment, you will remember that learning has always been more effective if it was fun and witty at the same time. By employing a degree of creativity when building your course, you can even end up having a good time yourself! Enjoying your work always helps and will certainly entice you to work faster and be more time-efficient.

Skills

More than just technical competencies on the course you'll be creating, you'll also need enough video production skills to create your video courses. While it is certainly possible to use your smartphone's camera to film yourself, there's more to it than that. It requires a post-shooting edit along with audio and video setting skills, at least if you want a good video on Udemy. Those are very technical things that you can probably learn over time but if you want to create a good course at the soonest possible time, better concentrate on the material and just get professional help for the video shoot and edits.

This is yet another opportunity to employ the services of freelancers to help you on your project. There is an abundance of video editors and audio mixers working as freelancers online, and a lot of them are real experts. For this, refer back to freelance websites we mentioned before, the likes of Upwork and Freelancer. You can divvy up the task and take on the writing or some other aspect of the work or you can delegate the whole thing to a professional. Based on your budget, time, and skills, you'll know best how to organize.

A lot of times, you can also look to schools for students who are majoring in graphic and video production. You can employ students for free or for much cheaper rates than professionals (some students are just as good as the professionals) in exchange for a project added to their portfolio or other forms of compensation. You also need to make sure your video portrays your personality as an individual and is not a lukewarm, dull interpretation of what you assume all online classes must be like.

Use enthusiasm and animate yourself so that your passion and interest will rub off on your students and give people more of an incentive to browse through and take more of your courses. It is much more interesting to watch an individual who is passionate about a topic than it is to watch someone who is not, or doesn't seem to be, interested in what they are teaching or talking about.

If you do possess fair skills in video editing and effects, be confident, because that personal touch only you can give just may be the factor that makes your course all that much more attractive and relatable.

HOW TO MAKE MONEY FROM UDEMY

It is pretty simple to do this. Start by creating a good course or outline of the things you want to cover in your course. When done, do not finalize it yet. Have someone else run through them, preferably someone who is not familiar with your course topic. That way, you get feedback on whether or not it is clear and understandable or too technical. Someone who is interested in the topic of your course and knows little to nothing about it will always be the perfect tester. If they have learned a considerable amount from your course and found it very comprehensible and instructive, then congratulations, because your course is a quality one!

Then make a video of yourself going through the whole course and have other people view it first so you can get objective feedback on whether or not it is clear and understandable. More than just the contents of the course, you'll also have to present them in a way that your enrollees can understand. After all, they expect to learn from your course, so you should give them their money's worth.

When you get enough good feedback about it, it is time to shoot the final video for your course. Do not scrimp on quality here. Invest in professional audio and video production if shooting and editing videos is not your skill and concentrate on what you do best — delivering your course. You do not want to end up half-doing two things. It is better to commit fully to one part of the work and see it through to quality, and just leave the other part to a pro.

Do not forget that you can make your course available for free! This is certainly something to consider with small-time projects as you begin building your reputation. Feedback is almost as important as the income itself. The relationship between positive feedback and increased revenue is not merely correlation, it is a guarantee.

If you are not in a rush and can take your sweet time building up this business, you might want to make your first course, or a couple of them, free. This way you minimize your risk of developing a bad reputation for seeking money for low-quality content.

At this point, it is pretty much assumed that you already have an account with Udemy. If not, go ahead and register. For more information about it, go directly to their site and check out their requirements and policies. I'm sure you read the Terms of Use Agreements whenever you set up an account anywhere on the Internet, but make sure you do the same here. After all, you are trying to make money on Udemy, so it helps to be well aware and informed about the ins and outs of the website.

Once you have an account, it is time to upload your course. But it doesn't end there; it is best to promote it outside of Udemy too. Marketing your course within the site will be easy with Udemy. There are personalized promotion programs in place already, so you will not have to get involved in that. This provides a lot of room for you to focus on outside promotion to an even wider range of people. You can promote it on social media and search engine optimization, among others. With social media in particular, you can either post it on your personal account — asking your friends to "share" the post — or use Facebook's paid advertisements.

If you already have an email list built up, you can also promote it there, assuming that it is consistent with the particular niche on which the list was built on. Imagine if your course was on a particular skill related to the niche your email list is built upon. This would mean that on top of the other content or products you are marketing through that list, you can now promote your course, which may be teaching students to do that which you do within the niche your subscribers care about. How awesome would that be?

And that's it! You're good to go!

ADVANCES IN STRATEGIES

Tips to keep in mind are providing quality content, abstaining from any slang terms or profanity, and maintaining a professional image. People look at nearly everything, especially when someone is on camera. Anything even slightly off with the individual, such as a stain on the shirt or a large tattoo, could take away from the quality of the course. You need to be aware that you are the image of your business; showing your professionalism in the way you carry yourself, speak and teach can keep people coming back for more because they feel as though the knowledge you are providing is valuable.

Whether you are looking to boost your own knowledge by taking advantage of the offerings on the Udemy or you want to become an instructor on the site, either direction will earn money in the long run. Knowledge creates ideas that you can turn into money and creating valuable courses and content creates the potential for knowledge that will be bought by individuals seeking knowledge in a particular field or area.

Chapter 8
Dividend-Paying Stocks

Stocks are a fantastic way to build a fortune for yourself. With the right investment strategies and financial capital, stocks have the potential to turn the average Joe into a millionaire over time, and at a faster rate than other passive incomes. A lot of us assume that the stock market is off limits for us because we either lack what we believe to be the required education, access, or prestige. Most of us do not realize that the stock market is not only available to everyone, but it is also easily accessible for everyone.

When attempting to dip your fingers into the stock market industry, it would be wise to conduct a fair amount of research on what the stock market is, what you are looking to gain (are you going for high risk or low risk?), and whether or not you have the funds to spare at the time. Some people put money aside for a while to build up enough cushion to invest in the stock market without losing the money they need for survival. The stock market won't make you a millionaire overnight, so investing money that you need to pay bills wouldn't be wise.

The stock market, though easily accessible, is a monster. Spreading across the globe, this market essentially connects the world of business at several central hubs throughout the world. There are several types of trading strategies people take on; establishing which one you would like to pursue is critical. Some people choose to dabble in the stock market once a month or so, checking their investments progression and selling current stocks or buying additional stocks. Some people choose to day-trade; these are the types of traders who work on Wall Street. A high volume of money is required to move stocks daily; it is also very risky.

One of the safest ways to use the stock market is to invest in a variety of different stocks in companies that you believe to be up and coming. There are established companies that are also safe to invest in but, for the most reward, it's best to invest in companies who haven't already taken off; then, when they do, you get the highest return on your stocks.

HOW TO GET STARTED

In order to begin investing, you need to decide if you want to research potential companies yourself or if you want the help of a financial advisor. Financial advisors will give you advice on what companies to invest in, along with advice on where to invest future earnings. If you choose to research companies yourself, check out some of the big-name financial websites like Fidelity or Scottrade. These sites will help you set up a profile with your initial investment and let you build lists of potential companies you would like to invest in.

You can create "watch lists" that will watch different stocks and keep track of the changes, alerting you if any of them shift in your favor. These sites will also help keep you organized and offer financial advice on which moves to take next, based on your trading style. Once you create a watch list, you can do more in-depth research on the companies you are watching, to see if they have been steadily progressing or slowly declining. Researching each business will give you a good indicator of the future prospects of the business and if it is going to give you a return on your money.

Keep in mind that using the stock market is not going to make you a millionaire instantly. Instead, it is going to build your income over time, giving you a decent-sized financial cushion that you can use to reinvest or withdraw by selling your stocks and collecting your earnings.

HOW DOES THE STOCK MARKET MAKE MONEY?

This was probably your first question. The stock market doesn't make passive money in the sense that the money is readily available as your stock's value increases. Instead, the stock market constantly changes, alerting you when there is a change in your stocks, giving you a heads-up in case you want to sell.

Essentially, you purchase stock in a company (think of it as a share) that you think is going to continue to grow. We are going to pretend the price is set at $7 a stock. You purchase 100 stocks at $7, making your total investment $700. Now, you go on about your life throughout the years, checking up on the company regularly and making sure the company is still functioning, and the stock prices aren't dropping. Occasionally, businesses have a few bad months, sometimes bad years; this means you have to decide if you want to stick with the company through the bad years or bail out and reinvest in a different company.

Let's say the $7 stocks drop down to $5, meaning your total investment as of now has lost money. The $700 you invested is now only $500. Unfortunately, this is the risk you have to take. However, another year passes, you decide to not sell your shares and stay with the company, a new CEO is brought in and completely redirects the company. The shares of the company begin to increase because of new products being released. You check your stocks and see that your stocks are now worth $10 apiece. Your initial investment of $700 is now $1000, meaning you have made a profit of $300. You stick with the company for the next five years, and the company's stocks have increased in price and are now worth $25 a share. You have now made a profit of $1,800. You can choose to sell your stocks and take the total amount earned: $2,500 - $700 initial investment = $1,800 profit.

In some cases, company's stocks can start out this low and skyrocket over years to being worth several hundred a share. Just imagine if you invested 300 stocks at $10 a share. After eight years pass, the company's stocks are now worth $435 a share. Your initial $3,000 investment has now reached $130,500, giving you a total profit of $127,500. Reinvesting a quarter of that money back into the stock market could make you even more money in the long run.

ADVANCES IN STRATEGIES

When playing the stock market, you need to pay careful attention to the companies you are investing in by watching them and setting up alerts so that you are notified if the stock drops below the purchase price. You need to maintain a high level of self-discipline, because a lot of people tend to panic and sell their stocks when they get closer to dropping below the purchase price. Selling may seem like the best idea, but it is actually going to cause the price of the stock to drop even more if everyone starts selling. Businesses have good and bad days, weeks, months, even years. One bad day shouldn't determine whether or not you sell your stocks. In fact, sticking with the company through the bad times may pay off big in the end when the stocks skyrocket again.

Keeping a good head on your shoulders and not panicking is the key to making good, logical decisions instead of decisions based on fear of the unknown.

The stock market is a great way to have your income build over time, giving you a great financial cushion for your future, in the case of emergency, or in case you need to make a large purchase of some sort. The amount of money that can build up throughout your lifetime is incredible and it is all based on the amount you invest initially and over time. Using a good model and taking a percentage of your earnings and reinvesting it back into the market in various other businesses can help to build your income substantially over time. People who do not reinvest a percentage of what they make risk losing it all if they have invested in just one company or they risk losing out on thousands of potential dollars.

Simon Wolf

Chapter 9
Miscellaneous Options

In addition to the previously mentioned ways of making a passive income, there are lots of other ways, as well. Many people aren't aware of the large number of options and ways to make money aside from having a regular 9-5 job; they are virtually endless. For those who enjoy their current profession, or thrive in a 9-5 setting, there are many ways to generate passive income on the side and there are many options for generating passive income that require less involvement than the aforementioned methods. Of course, a smaller amount of work and time put into your method of earning passive income will result in smaller profits. The methods covered in this chapter are great for those who are looking supplement their main source of passive income, make some extra pocket money, or kick-start a saving account.

Stock Photography

We are in a world where images and videos are taking over. Now more than ever, people are taking hundreds of pictures a day of a variety of different things. If you ever thought about making money from the photos that you take, you are in luck. A lot of people take photos of various subjects: nature, water, people, places, buildings, designs, and changing weather patterns. After taking pictures, some of these people put them up for sale on a website or sell from a booth at art shows and festivals. In a world where the Internet rules, a lot of businesses, books, organizations, everything really, needs unique, quality photos for a variety of uses.

For example, imagine that a company is posting an article on its website about coffee. A lot of people think you can just go online and Google keywords such as *coffee* or *coffee cup* and use their favorite image from Google images to place on the website. The only way in which this is legal is to contact the original source for the photograph, asking permission to use the photograph, or to cite the original owner and source below the photograph. Doing this will not only make the photograph look unprofessional and cluttered with words, but there is also the possibility that millions of other people are also viewing that photo on Google images, making it less than unique when seen on your website.

So, in short, businesses will pay for stock photography so they can be sure that the purchased image is available for use and is unique. This might be hard to believe, but there are many sites where photographers can upload their pictures and receive payment for them if they choose, though most prefer to sell through their own website to avoid incurring extra fees. What is great about digital photography is that you rarely have to print out the images, cutting back the costs significantly. Most of the cost incurred for photography was from the materials needed to frame the image, the ink, and paper to print the image, and other necessary materials.

YouTube Videos

Making YouTube videos or podcasts is a great way to make money as well. To get started, you need a webcam and a microphone, along with something interesting to talk about. Some people do reaction videos to others people's videos or to certain things happening in the news; these are somewhat popular. A lot of people do funny videos where they talk about certain odd topics or rant about something that's bothering them. Some people do tutorials that instruct people on how to do certain things like makeup, crafts, mechanics, etc. This is a good market to get into, especially if there is something you are really good at. A lot of people look to YouTube to learn about anything, even changing a tire, so having a variety of tutorials to choose from gives people a lot of options.

Some people make videos telling stories about things they have encountered or chronicling something like cancer treatment or weight loss; it really depends on the individual and what you have to offer.

You can make money through YouTube in a few different ways. Having ad space on your YouTube channel and allowing ads to appear before your video and around your channel can help make money, especially if people click on these ads. Affiliate marketing by either marketing products or mentioning them in your videos is also a good way to make money because companies will pay for you to mention them. A lot of times, companies will send you free products to review on your channel or to wear during one of your videos.

Finally, you can make money by branding yourself and selling your own products. If you have a certain slogan or catch phrase that gets you a lot of subscribers, put them on t-shirts, coffee cups, and other types of products that people could give as gifts or use on a daily basis.

These can make money for you because, after you make videos, you can continue to make them or make a few in advance and schedule them to post at a certain time each week. As your videos are viewed and played, ads will be clicked, and merchandise will hopefully be bought, and money will trickle in.

Foreign Exchange Market (FOREX)

A lesser-known way to make quick income, with the risk of losing it just as quickly, is through the foreign exchange market. This market is defined as a "global decentralized market for the trading of currencies. This includes all aspects of buying, selling and exchanging currencies at current or determined prices. In terms of volume of trading, it is by far the largest market in the world." The foreign exchange market can be entered by anyone with any amount of money, though the highest returns are for individuals with higher investments.

What is difficult with the foreign exchange market is its high level of unpredictability. It is nearly impossible to tell which way the market will go and whether it will bounce back before the market of your choice closes. The markets are not all open at the same time. Different countries are open at different time periods:

- New York: 8:00 am EST – 12:00 noon EST
- Tokyo: 7:00 pm EST – 4:00 am EST
- Sydney: 5:00 pm EST – 2:00 am EST
- London: 3:00 am EST – 12:00 noon EST

Times overlap for different individuals, which is why the market is open all hours of the day, except Saturday and Sunday. Although a lot of the participants in the foreign exchange market are large international banks, there are also brokers at hedge funds and financial funds, as well as individual brokers. It can be difficult for individual brokers to make a large amount of money unless they have a lot to trade up front because of the amount of competition. Every event can change the way the market turns. There are two different types of trading techniques: technical trading and fundamental trading. The definitions of both are as follows:

Fundamental analysis: This is a method of evaluating securities by attempting to measure the intrinsic value of a stock. Fundamental analysts study everything from overall economy and industry conditions to the financial condition and management of companies. Fundamental trading may involve watching the news to see if there are any big events in the news, anything from meetings between government officials, to mass shootings and plane crashes, and minor things like holidays and speeches from higher-up officials.

Technical Analysis: This is the evaluation of securities by means of studying statistics generated by market activity, such as past prices and volume. Technical analysts do not attempt to measure a security's intrinsic value but instead use stock charts to identify patterns and trends that may suggest what a stock will do in the future. A lot of technical traders look far back into past charts to see and attempt to predict future patterns and directions. This can be difficult in certain markets and can be incredibly tedious, but it pays off if done correctly.

These techniques are polar opposites of one another, but using a combination of the two can be a most effective technique. You have to take into account not only the past trends for the day, but also look and see what is going on this day as opposed to previous years. For example, June 5, 2015, may show one value, but there was also a speech by an elected official who was addressing a recent violent act, whereas June 5, 2016, shows a value different than the previous year because there nothing historically significant happened on this day.

Tasks You Do Daily

There are other ways to make money doing things you already do daily. Some sites will actually pay you to shop on the Internet, play Internet games, take short surveys, etc. Anything that you normally do on the Internet could possibly be earning your money or savings. There are so many sites that offer such services that listing them in this book would be impossible, but they offer individual ways to make and save small amounts of money that can add up to a lot in the long term.

Real Estate

This is a risky market if you do not know what you are doing; it also takes a significant amount of financial investment to start, along with a mortgage that goes on your credit, potentially affecting it negatively if the mortgage is not paid on time. However, investing in the right property can be highly lucrative if you know where to purchase and what to look for. There are several ways you can go about purchasing an investment property.

Purchasing your first home with the intent to move out of it within a few years after fixing it up is a good start because, if you decide you do not want to take the risk to invest in other properties, you already have a home you enjoy and can stay in. It can be an issue if you sacrifice things you want in order to purchase your first home and then decide you do not want to move or purchase another home, because then you are stuck with the home you purchased, unless you decide to sell or rent down the road.

You can purchase a home with the intent of renting out the property immediately after purchase. When looking into purchasing this type of income property, you need to make sure the rent you are charging will cover the mortgage payment and any other bills and expenses. You will have to make sure the house is up to code and livable, safe, and pest-free. Establishing a security deposit is a good way to ensure that, should the tenant destroy the property before they leave, you have the financial means to repair things like windows and door knobs and perform other miscellaneous cosmetic projects.

Ideally, if you can purchase a large home and separate it into multiple units, this can generate even more income than a single-family home. Consider purchasing close to cities or large universities and colleges, because this will ensure that there will be potential renters year round, making it less likely you will go an extended period of time without a renter. After you accumulate enough properties, you can hire a maintenance employee who can respond to any maintenance calls on the property, taking the responsibility out of your hands. This gives you more time to enjoy the recurring income of your rental properties and search for more potential rental properties.

Having several rental properties is especially great after the homes are paid off because essentially nearly all of the rent collected is profit. There are other means of income such as buying a home, flipping it, and selling it for a higher profit, but this requires a lot of work and wouldn't be considered passive income because the money is made in one lump sum when the house is sold.

Become a referral source

Many small and local business offer incentives to those who bring in new business. These businesses often pay cash rewards to those who refer friends and help successfully generate new business through word of mouth.

Create a list of small businesses you frequent, then call up the owners and ask if they offer referral bonuses. Businesses that typically offer these bonuses are accountants, landscapers, electricians, plumbers, carpet cleaners, pool builders, and many more. A few phone calls can easily result in generating a passive income from the simple act of making recommendations to friends and family.

Many workplaces also offer referral bonus programs. Check with your work place to see if you can benefit financially from referring new customers, or even employees.

Become a brand ambassador

In this day and age, startup companies are running rampant in the business world. Many of these fresh new companies are using aggressive marketing campaigns. These campaigns often employ brand ambassadors to spread the word about their company and, in turn, pay them for generating new business.

For example, companies like Lyft and Uber offer unique coupon codes for you to give out to friends, family, and even businesses. When a customer uses your coupon code, you earn money. It is possible to generate quite a bit of income this way. Posting your unique code on sites like Facebook, Twitter, Instagram, and other forms of social media is a great way to spread your code around without doing much work or spending any money. Purchasing posters or cards with your unique code and handing them out or leaving them at places of business can greatly increase your chances of earning money from referrals, but requires a bit more work and a small investment.

There are companies like Forever Living Products or Avon who require you to sell their products and build up your own network of sales people during the process. To begin with, you will really have to market and sell the products and, of course, use them yourself. Once you begin to generate your own regular sales, you can start to recruit people who will work under you to do exactly the same. You will earn commissions from their sales, as well as bonuses if your team reaches certain targets. Yes, this is hard work to begin with but, once you have created your dream team, you will be on a smooth course with passive income from the sales of your team members. The trick here is in building a team that will be successful and offering them the tools and support to be successful. This may not be for everyone as it does involve a lot of cold calling, speaking to strangers, and, of course, Internet marketing, but in the end it will be worth it because of the passive income you will earn.

Go online and research which companies offer the most lucrative brand ambassador programs. Chances are you'll find more than one avenue for this and will be able to generate income through multiple brand ambassador programs. There are many companies with online stores who offer affiliate programs and, even if you do not have a blog or website, you can still earn from sales to clients you verbally direct to purchase through your link. Yes, this will, of course, take much longer to generate a decent passive income but starting slowly is not always a bad thing. Once you realize that you can earn by getting people to purchase through your link, Internet marketing, blogs, and the like will follow. As you see your earning grow, you will be more receptive to the idea of using the Internet to promote your link.

Rent your unused space through Airbnb

Airbnb is a fairly new company that allows individuals to turn their homes into hotels. Airbnb offers travelers around the world a cheaper alternative to established hotels. When you become an Airbnb member, you can earn money by renting out parts of your home, such an unused guest room, to guests.

For those located in or near a popular city or in the vicinity of a popular tourist attraction, Airbnb can provide a great source of income. Airbnb income in high-traffic areas will be much higher than income for those located in rural areas or small towns. Airbnb income is also based on the size and condition of the space you have to offer.

If you have space in your home that continuously goes unused and you do not mind the company of new people, Airbnb may provide you with an easy source of passive income.

Buy a blog

While creating your own blog from the ground up takes quite a bit of time and dedication, purchasing a blog that already generates web traffic and income is a far less time-consuming option. While some financial investment is required to purchase a blog, it is often cheaper to purchase a blog that has already developed a following than to develop one from scratch.

The average blog uses Google Adsense to generate monthly income through ads placed by Google on the sites. Many pre-established blogs also earn income through affiliate marketing. Once you find and purchase a blog, you will be seeing revenue from both of these avenues. Blogs typically sell for 24 times their monthly revenue, so your investment depends on how much the blog you choose is already generating.

While many blogs contain "evergreen" content that continuously generates income even after the site has become inactive, a great way to boost traffic and revenue is to add fresh content frequently. Adding relevant content to an already developed blog is very easy. If you do not want to write or create content yourself, outsourcing for articles and graphics can cost very little, yet benefit your blog in a big way.

Buying a blog takes a bit more work and money than some of the passive income methods above, but earning an extra $250-$400 a month without a major time investment could easily benefit your bank account.

Pay off a credit card

While paying off a credit card doesn't necessarily generate income, it does eliminate a fixed expense, which, in turn, creates passive income. If you owe $10,000 on a credit card, and are making a payment of $200 a month, eliminating this payment will generate $2,400 a year in income.

A great way to make paying off credit cards more manageable is by transferring current balances to a 0%

APR card. A quick Google search can pull up a long list of promotional offers from credit card companies that offer 0% APR for up to 15 months.

Utilize cash-back rewards on credit cards

If you are already using credit cards, cash back rewards are a fantastic way to generate passive income. Top rewards cards can earn you anywhere from 1% to 5% cash back on purchases, which can easily help you earn money, save money and keep your debt at bay.

Most cash-back cards require you to spend a certain amount of money within an allotted time in order for you to earn the rewards. For example, one of the top cash-back cards requires customers to spend $4,000 within 90 days in order to receive $500 cash back. While this may seem like a lot of spending for some, paying monthly bills and expenses on your credit card can quickly amount to the spending requirement, then you can immediately pay off what you've spent.

Taking advantage of cash-back credit cards is a good passive income method for those who stay on top of debt. If you are someone who falls behind on credit card debt, this avenue may hurt your income more than help.

Utilize cash-back rewards or credit coupons from retail stores and supermarkets

Many retail stores and supermarkets offer cash back points on purchases in order to draw the customers into their stores. You fill in a short form, are issued a card, and each time you purchase and swipe that card, you earn points which are redeemable for goods at that store. If you have a favorite supermarket or retail store, try to use only those stores and cash in on the points system. This is not what would normally be considered an income, but you do earn "money" simply for doing your weekly or monthly grocery shopping and that will in the long term save you money as your points grow.

Register for a points system with your credit card - voyager miles or similar companies offer great points for purchasing with your card.

Many credit card companies and banking facilities now offer programs for which you can register. Voyager Miles is a terrific one where you earn Voyager Miles while doing monthly payments with your credit card. Let the points accumulate and you can finally take that flight to your holiday destination and your flight is covered by the miles you have accumulated. There are other programs that work on the same principle, but they allow you to book accommodation and even car rentals with your points. Of course, it must be with their selected partners but hey, you get to go on holiday and you have already paid for it. This should only be used by people who religiously pay their cards and budget properly, using their cards with caution and responsibility. No use running up your credit card for a flight and hotel room. If that is the case, you may as well just have paid for it using the card.

Advertise events

If you are well versed in the use of social media sites and have loads of followers, then this is perfect for you. Offer to advertise events through your social media channels for a percentage of ticket sales generated, or even a fixed amount per event. This is fun and easy thing to do if you are someone who is outgoing and adventurous. Select events that suit your hobbies and interests and market them on all your social media platforms.

This is a great way for young adults to get into the passive income market. Marketing dances, festivals, or music shows are perfect ways for young adults to make some extra holiday money and enjoy the shows themselves.

Create an iPad or iPhone app

Phew! This sounds like it will cost a fortune but a simple information-based app really doesn't cost all that much to create. There are plenty of online do-it-yourself sites to help you create your own basic app. All you really need is a great idea and information that everybody is after. Get your thinking cap on and, if it is great, you'll make some passive income when people download your app and use it. Some time and imagination and you are on your way to earning some pennies.

YouTube Series

Create a YouTube how-to series for something that is used by people every day. You see so many videos of how to apply makeup or paint your nails properly and these are all great, because people want to know how to do that kind of thing. Think up a fantastic idea, research, speak to people, get your series in motion in your mind and on paper. Have a few episodes lined up beforehand to keep the momentum going.

Get your drama gear out and perhaps a friend who really wants to be an actress and get that plan in motion. Record the first one and make it brilliant. If you get viewers hooked first time around, they will definitely be back for your weekly installments and views, view, views will eventually start earning you some passive income. This does take up some time but, if you do these videos, it should be because you love it and not because it is a job. Remember you will earn even if viewers view your early videos and you might already be on episode 50 (here's hoping).

Get that webcam or digital recorder out and charged and let the show begin.

Buy and rent equipment

Invest in some expensive equipment that people often need to use for one time only — perhaps certain camera equipment or music playing equipment. Market these items online and get your diary packed with rentals week after week. There is obviously some capital outlay and some marketing work involved, but the rest of the income is pretty much passive income. A bit of marketing and you are on your way. Once word gets out and your customers are satisfied, they will keep coming back and probably send their friends there too.

Buy and rent formal dresses

Invest in some great gowns that girls could hire for proms or weddings. Shop around and you will find some bargain deals. Often girls do not want to splurge on a made-to-order dress that they will probably never wear again and opt for the cheaper option of hiring. This will take some initial cash outlay, obviously dry cleaning costs, and, of course, an investment in marketing. Market in the right places and your customers will be lining up down the street. Advertise on school websites for prom dresses, start a blog, or advertise using social media.

Design

Get those creative juices flowing and design your way to a fairly passive income. Use the many programs and sites available to design funky, fun and fashionable designs that can be used on anything: designs for T-shirts, designs for mugs, designs for clocks. Make sure the designs are completely original and target different markets. Set up a site, load your designs, and wait for those valuable clicks to purchase. This option will take time perhaps once a month where you will need to sit down and create new designs to add to your site. If you really are creative by nature, this shouldn't be work at all, rather spending time doing what you love. As your designs become more popular, add to the categories. Perhaps include a request blog on your site to see what your customers and viewers are looking for. A truly fun way to make some much needed money. Do some hard work at the beginning of the month and you can watch as your designs are ordered and paid for during the rest of the month.

The customers are purchasing the designs that can be used on different items and not the printed products so you will have an online business that provides you with time to focus on what you love and make money at the same time.

A little work and you are on your way to a successful passive income.

There are really so many things that you could do to earn a passive income. Yes, they initially involve quite a bit of set up and work and some involve some outlay of cash up front, but they are well worth it if you are doing something you love.

Open your mind, explore your hobbies and the things you love to do and you will definitely find a way to use that and turn it into a lucrative passive income.

The key to a great passive income opportunity is to put in the necessary hours to set up your marketing strategies properly to start with. Once that is set up, you can really sit back and watch your wallet fill up. Of course, you have to have a product, service, or idea that everybody wants to get their hands on so it will surely pay to research and check what is popular in the market place at the time.

Try to steer clear of things that have been done too often, as the market will already be flooded with these sorts of ideas. If you do select something that has been done over and over, be sure to add your own personal twist to it and in this way make it completely different.

Ideas on the market obviously do work or there wouldn't be so many people trying the same thing. So sometimes sticking with what you know works and is a good idea but, as I said, you need to make your product or service stand out from the crowd so that they select you over all the other similar sites.

With so many social media platforms and free-to-advertise sites available today, you have no excuse for poor marketing. Passive income depends on you and how much you put into your marketing strategy, how and whom to target and, of course, your price range.

To earn a passive income successfully, you really have to think outside the box and explore options you would never have thought of. Remember that great ideas are not put into action overnight and success will certainly not be overnight. Persevere and keep at it; your initial hard work and time will pay off if you are confident in what you are offering and original in your presentation of the products or services.

Be passionate about your choice, use the products or wear the items as extra advertising. Promoting something you use or wear yourself is so much easier than trying to sell something you have only read about. Passion is one of the keys to success in business and is sometimes taken for granted. If you love what you are doing, you will do it so much better.

Always keep an eye on market trends and, if need be, change your strategy from time to time. Keep the content constantly fresh and new. People do not want to keep coming back to a site just to view what they have seen the last ten times. Add new items regularly and make these items stand out in your advertising to show that your site has been updated.

Creating a successful passive income empire will free up time for you to spend with your family, to learn new skills through hobbies, and to meet new people. Time is something none of us has enough of these days. Hectic lifestyles, work, traffic, we hardly ever have quality time for our families or even ourselves. Get out of the rut you are stuck in and start creating your own future.

Passive income can be an amazing opportunity for anybody who is looking to take control of their own lives and finances. These days, in an economic climate that is less than favorable and employment on the decrease, it is possibly the best time to take a chance on yourself and make things happen in your life. There is no time like the present to jump in feet first; you will soon realize that you can float on your own but hard work and dedication are required in the beginning phases. Do not think that the path is going to be carefree and labor-free.

Simon Wolf

Conclusion

Thank you for buying this book. Now that you've learned how to earn passive income via the Internet, you're ready to increase your income without having to break your back — or the bank.

However, knowing is just half the battle. The other half is applying what you learned, so I highly encourage you to start applying the knowledge you've acquired here or learn more about the systems I have outlined. Take the initiative. Find which method works best for you and tackle it head on. Conduct your own further research. Talk to someone in your life who hasn't taken steps toward creating a passive income. Any step toward generating your own income is step in the right direction. One way or the other, you'll be acting on what you've learned. By doing nothing, you're just left with an entertaining book and mostly, trivia.

Action is the name of the game here. Although it may happen once or twice in a lifetime, you still can't count on good things coming spontaneously. Sure, there are many who get lucky, but by developing your own passive income you won't have to sit by the wayside praying for something magical to happening. You'll make your own magic! Besides, it is better to spend this "once or twice" allowance on harder things in life than work, like the dreaded relationships!

The thing least likely to come on its own is freedom, independence. This has become undeniably true for the world we occupy today. Why would I say that? Well, I say it because they do not want you to be free and work for yourself. This is not some conspiracy theory either; it is rather the nature of the beast called "the economy." Now, I'm not saying that "work" or "jobs" are bad things. I'm positive that there are plenty of people who are more than happy with their regular line of employment. Neither am I promoting laziness; far from it, God forbid! If you have learned anything from this book it is that passive income, despite its name, will require determination, effort, and time — work! But the trick to this business, or rather the whole purpose of it, is to put that work into a thing of your own. It is building this system with the aim of it working for you. It is paving your way to a life that may have seemed impossible before. It is moving you in the direction of full financial freedom.

In any business, someone has to work for it to run and be profitable, but here, it is about making the technology be that "someone." It is about harnessing the limitless potential of the Internet, which we take completely for granted nowadays. And rest assured — the Internet is here to stay, and overstay. Computers, smart phones, tablets and other technological staples are here for the long haul. They will only continue to improve and become more and more necessary. Opportunity will continue to arise from these advancements. This machine, this entire eco-system, will continue to grow, improve, and become ever more accessible throughout the world. Developing a business built on the foundation of technology and the Internet is a way to assure you will never be without a source of income. The only way it'll go away is in the case of all-out nuclear Armageddon or an asteroid collision. Of course, in that event, we will all be dead, so it really is not anything to be anxious about as far as the passive income business is concerned.

In retrospect, the striving to be one's own boss and work as little as possible for a decent level of income has been with us since ancient times. As a matter of fact, it is in our very primal nature to strive to achieve results with the least amount of effort. If I were to run really wild with it, I'd say this instinct is precisely the reason we invented tools, discovered fire, and even started drinking coffee. It is all about efficiency and comfort.

The race toward efficiency can be observed in all walks of life and human affairs. Though the media often warns us of a failing economy that makes it impossible for those not born into money to find success, that is simply untrue. There is no such thing as a shortage of opportunity. There is no cap or limit on the number of successful people in the world. Even during the Great Depression, the absolute worst economic slump in American history, numerous people came out on top, making a fortune for themselves despite the country's terrible financial situation. Even in the darkest of times, people sought means of building efficient, comfortable lives. Naturally, this is why the means to achieve such a life are more advanced now than ever before, and will continue to evolve at ever-increasing rates.

The benchmark of this progress is, of course, the Internet. The Internet has facilitated all forms of business on an unprecedented level. In fact, its impact is so powerful that even the competition, which is at an all-time high in today's economy, cannot stop you from succeeding if your focus is strong enough. The monopoly of powerful multinational corporations has become threatened by emerging independent markets and will probably continue to be. This is happening in quite a few industries, and it is all thanks to the many forms of accessible tech: affordable and fast Internet, open-source software, and countless other tools for all sorts of tasks, which are getting cheaper and cheaper as our choices expand further. For example, just think about the resources, connections, and even manpower, required to develop a video game about 25 to 35 years ago? Computers the size of Mack trucks and teams of wildly intelligent people used to take decades just to create a basic game. Nowadays, practically anyone can acquire the tools and the wisdom to do what was considered almost a marvel back then, the very cutting edge it used to be!

Looking back at the beginning of this book, I'm sure that, after reading through all of this, you see clearly what I meant when I rebuked those among us who fear and shun technology. It is a sin against ourselves, against our potential, to cast technological advancement aside as something that's detrimental to our livelihood, something that's out to get us.

The people who spout such claims and platitudes are either too afraid to take those first steps or are malicious and do not want you to succeed. Because, let me tell you, the only thing that technology really threatens is our shackles and the ability of others to control our destiny. Pay no mind to naysayers, do take advice where available and learn, learn, learn, but do not let yourself be discouraged by those who only want to hamper progress because of their own insecurities. Luckily they are not hard to identify! You can tell a cynic without a cause easily by looking at where they stand, or more precisely stagnate. Online passive income is real; well, it has been real for a long time, but it is more tangible now than ever.

One thing I cannot stress enough is how difficult it will be to begin. Many of the options listed require learning curves and, though simple, are hard to throw yourself into without having a lot of time. Most of you reading this have full-time jobs, so you physically do not have the time to spend all day working on a website or scouring the Internet for products, or even making YouTube videos. This means that, although passive income is possible for you, it is going to take a lot more time than you might think to begin churning a profit. For example, with FOREX trading, it can take 6-12 months before you even begin to start generating a profit and this is if you haven't lost all of your money by then.

For people looking to write for KDP, writing ebooks may seem easy until you realize the sheer volume of words a book requires, and how difficult it can be to use proper sentence structure, grammar, and punctuation. If you do not want to write the books yourself, but want to pay someone to do them for you, then you are investing your money in another individual to write your book without knowing what the outcome will be. You are also taking the risk of not having a return on your investment if you do not sell enough books to break even or profit.

Working for yourself, as I stated before, is much harder than working for someone else. Waking up in the morning at a decent hour, getting ready as if going to work or to an office, and sitting down to work takes a lot of motivation and can be mentally exhausting just to stay focused at home. Some people choose to work at coffee shops or choose to rent an office in a building just to have a change of scenery, because being at home all day can make people begin to go stir-crazy. A lot of people think working at home is easier than working for someone else, when it is actually the opposite. I can guarantee that, if you are motivated enough to successfully use some of the tools this book has listed or that the Internet has to offer to earn passive income, then you are more than prepared to work from home and be successful.

So take the next step toward successfully earning passive income! May the odds be ever in your favor!

Remember that fortune does favor the brave! Cheers!

www.ingramcontent.com/pod-product-compliance
Lightning Source LLC
Chambersburg PA
CBHW070234190526
45169CB00001B/176